LET THE HEART LEAD

Let the Heart Lead
by Priyal Bansal

First Published in India in 2020
Inkfeathers Publishing
New Delhi 110095

ISBN 978-81-946199-4-9

www.inkfeathers.com

LET THE HEART LEAD

Priyal Bansal

Inkfeathers Publishing

www.inkfeathers.com

CONTENTS

Introduction *vii*

PART I: GIVE YOUR THOUGHTS AVATAR

LAW OF ATTRACTION 1

MAKE THE BEST USE 5

MANIFESTATION SKILLS 11

UNRAVEL THE TRUTHS 19

PART II: KNOW YOUR COMRADES

ANGELS AND COMPANIONS 27

GUARDIAN ANGELS 29

SOUL MATES 35

TWIN FLAMES 43

SPIRIT ANIMALS 51

KINDRED SPIRITS 63

PART III: INVIGORATE YOU

SPIRITUAL AWAKENING 73

MORNING ALARM 77

FAIRYTALE 81

DARK NIGHT 85

OBLIVION 89

GROUNDED 93

AFTERLIFE 97

TOP 7 QUESTIONS 103

Acknowledgements 107

About the Author 109

INTRODUCTION

Before starting this book, I would like you to chant "OM" five times, inhaling and exhaling with it.

OM, OM, OM, OM, OM!

Om may be simple, but it is also powerful. There is a great deal of meaning packed into it. The sound and vibration of the mantra has a calming feel to it which makes it the perfect way to achieve focus as you do meditation. There are thousands of mantras in Hindu and Buddhist texts but trying to condense them to any shortlist is always a challenge.

But have you ever wondered what makes these mantras so strong and effective? Collect all the curiosity and dive into the book to get your answers!

Well, being a teenager, I have encountered both the spiritual and not so spiritual side of the society and my observations say that there is always a sense of peace and accomplishment on the spiritual side.

I do not claim that the second half is not spiritual; the only difference is that they are still in slumber. They are a life. They have a soul. But they are still not conscious about having it. Spirituality usually involves the belief in a higher form of intelligence and consciousness running the universe, as well as life after death. It exists to satisfy the deeper human thirst and craving for meaning, peace, mystery, and truth.

When I talk about spirituality in this second half of the world, I see, these people are conditioned to understand it as something which asks you to leave every material thing you hold and go on with the search to enlightenment. But do you expect a 16-year-old to find enlightenment?—Surely no!

And that is why I say that spirituality deals with the heart and mind sync. How can we expect to give up materials when we live in a materialistic world? All we require is faith in heart and control in mind.

Spirituality is the knowledge that allows human beings to accomplish their perfection, meaning the state in which their existing nature is realized. It can be considered as a complete experimental science that can guide us towards true knowledge of our rights and duties and motivates us to perform them.

I want you to read this book so that you know you are divinely loved, you are immensely blessed and everything going around you is what you need. Having a strong spiritual outlook may help you find meaning in life's difficult circumstances. And I stand with this for the whole of my life.

Now, you must be wondering why you should read my work? Or why you should trust me? Of course, there are so many books and information out about this topic. And I will say that this is why you should read my work. I state every aspect of the topic I know. I do not stand by keeping you in fairyland.

Another dynamic you will face while reading the book is that it would make you fall in love with yourself. While I was writing this book, I have encountered many cases related to anxiety, depression, and suicide. I wonder how I can stop this because my mission is to create and teach. I want to build a world full of people who love themselves so unconditionally before anyone.

We are humans and it is easy for us to forget that there is always a universal power that is here to protect and guide us. Everything we experience in life is a teaching. Guides are here to remind us how to get back on track. To show us that we are loved, and we are here to play, create, nurture, and connect with them.

To grow and develop, humans need what we have called "divine warmth" and "divine light." Divine light refers to spiritual knowledge and to ensemble authentic ethical principles of divine origin which enables us to achieve sufficient comprehension and thereby to internally assimilate them. Whereas divine warmth, refers to divine love, the love that we feel towards the Creator which generates within us the necessary motivation and energy for action and generates self-love.

There is a very strong drive in many of us to evolve, to improve, to push the boundaries, and reach our full potential. The drive which pushes you to continuously grow and learn, live a life authentic to our truth, develop our mind, cultivate virtues, and expand our consciousness. I want to trigger that path; I want to collect your blessings and I want to grow with you.

We as humans portray our cruel side today and forget that we are not conditioned to hate. We were made to spread love and this race was made to support each other through this journey. I want to help and tell that someone has got your back.

Spirituality also teaches us that "evil" has no substantive existence, but rather these are the results from the dysfunction of responsible beings such as humans. Therefore, we have a duty to fight against evil, but this does not state that we should perceive others as being evil or to wish ill upon them.

It is in this context that forgiveness and forbearance find true meaning, and strength and empathy become important.

And nonetheless, at least we get confidence that by the end, it wouldn't matter if we win or not, we get faith and love. Every mechanism that we are using to navigate. To do the work we are doing is a natural mechanism or expression that occurs normally in our daily lives. This is the backup mechanism from the universe and the reason they do it like this is so that they can be sure it will still happen, or start to happen, even without conscious interference.

Thereby, by building the mechanisms into our normal day to day life expression, we could be sure the shift would start—even if none of us had woken up already into the spiritual world.

Diving into one's consciousness and exploring other aspects of reality is something that speaks about our thirst for knowledge, experience, and adventure. Learning about the mysteries of life and nature, exploring the sacred and living with a sense of wonder.

The urge to serve people on a deeper level, making a big difference in their lives and society in general, and helping the upliftment of humanity becomes vital to us.

Some of these things may not speak to you at all, while you would feel a great attraction for other things. It's all good. That is why there are different paths out there, to match seekers of different temperaments, stages of development, values, and goals. For me, there was always a pull towards truth, transcendence, enlightenment, but I can see I got benefits in all the other areas as well.

In a way, all these drives have one thing in common: they show we are not satisfied with only the material side of life, and we wish to move beyond this limitation and explore ourselves.

Suffering is the initial door of spirituality for many people. But when our mind depends on external and material things for happiness, its experience of happiness will be unreliable, impermanent—just like external causes. Suffering is considered a mental phenomenon, and spiritual practices are a means to transform one's mind and life, and it is a wise way of seeking a better life.

Whether you are on the top of the wheel of material life or at the bottom, there is an underlying sense of dissatisfaction, limitation, and emptiness within. There is some form of existential anxiety and stress. Some people are sensitive to this, others aren't, or they try to fill this up by chasing external goals endlessly.

Spirituality is searching for meaning, purpose and direction in life. It fulfils our need to have a foundation for living, a path or way of life in the light of a larger context. It speaks to the need to be "aligned" with something bigger than our ego, mind, and individual life. Need to be aligned to our higher self, aligned to our soul.

Yet so many people learn about it, understand it, try to apply it, and have trouble. Today, so many people are unhappy, depressed, and in ruins with many aspects of their life- be it finances, and relationships, etc. So, I want to spread the word on this powerful force and in a very concise and easy way, I want to guide you through the process of spirituality, and how to use it to your advantage to create the life you truly desire.

I want to create that urge in you to search for every bit of peace you can have. I want to ignite the curiosity for the questions within you. I want you to experience all the joy you are missing upon.

Spiritual individuals strive toward a better life and consider personal growth and fulfilment as a central goal. It can be considered to be a path toward self-actualization because it requires people to focus on their internal values and work on becoming a better individual. And spiritual fellowship provides a sense of belonging, security, and community.

So, let's hold each other's hands and grow together into something unique because you and I have our blessings, our worth. Let's move towards our life purposes and ultimate pleasure. And let us use every pinch of power we have to attain an immensely beautiful world in and out.

Now again before diving into the book, chant OM!

Om, Om, Om, Om, Om!

PART I

GIVE YOUR THOUGHTS AVATAR

Believe and expect that it will deliver.

Feel it, allow it, you are the law giver.

All that we are is a result of what we have thought

But remember this is not about one single shot

Know that you and the source are one.

The source is the father, and you are the son.

Happiness is not a destination; it's a method of life

You'll not achieve it until and unless you strive.

~ Priyal Bansal

LAW OF ATTRACTION

Before starting this journey, I want you to think of those experiences where you wanted something so badly and you did everything wholeheartedly to achieve that, and you succeeded.

I am sure there would be many experiences. And also, you would be wondering about these business tycoons who have built such big mansions and have a million-dollar empire- how did they achieve that?

The entire secret to their success is the Law of attraction. Living in this century and reading my book surely reveals that you must have heard of this law but might not know what it is. The Law of Attraction is one of life's biggest mysteries. Very few people are fully aware of how much of an impact the Law of Attraction has on their day-to-day life. Whether we are doing it knowingly or unknowingly, every second of our existence, we are acting as human magnets sending out our thoughts and emotions and attracting back more of what we have put out.

Before I get into detail about this law I want to share its history in brief so, hundreds of years ago the Law of Attraction was first thought to have been taught to man by the immortal Buddha. It is believed he wanted it to be known that 'what you have become is what you have thought'. With the spread of this concept to western culture also came the term 'Karma', it is a belief that is popular throughout numerous societies. Thomas Troward, a thought leader who had a strong influence on today's beliefs of the Law of Attraction, claimed that thought precedes physical form. He believed, "The action of Mind plants that nucleus which, if allowed to grow undisturbed, will eventually attract to itself all the conditions necessary for its manifestation in outward visible form."

If you read the introduction you must know when I asked about the strength of the mantras. I asked you why are they so powerful and effective. The reason is the law of attraction. These mantras have existed for so many decades and they get stronger by each day. Among these mantras lie people's faith and trust, their energy, emotions. A whole lot of community put their faith and expectations and that is what makes them so strong. Energy is neither created, nor destroyed, neither has it taken birth nor it dies. The energy is conserved and so is happening with these affirmations and mantras.

This simple and easy-to-follow concept of law of attraction has been so popular among many for a large number of years. It demonstrates that the idea of the power of attraction is not new. The most challenging part of acknowledging and accepting the truth of what the Law of Attraction has to offer, is realizing that every single one of your decisions in life, good and bad have been shaped by you alone.

Now those who ask for if there are any scientific theories or proofs about this, and then tell them to search about the law of attraction in quantum physics! The work of quantum physicists during recent years has helped to shine greater light on the incredible impact that the power of the mind has on our lives and the universe in general. Under laboratory conditions, rapidly growing science has confirmed that every single thought you have is made up of energy and it has its unique frequency. And when this energy and frequency of your thought radiates out into the Universe, it tends to naturally interact with the material world.

At this point, you may still remain unconvinced that this principle—like attracts like—is a scientific one. It may still seem interwoven in magic and, therefore, unreal. Perhaps it's because we're talking about intangible concepts like thoughts and feelings. With gravity, an apple thrown up into the air falls onto the ground. You may not understand it, but you can visibly and immediately experience the effects.

MAKE THE BEST USE

I am sure you must have been very fascinated by this whole concept till now but if you ask someone who knows about this concept then you are likely to hear that, "go manifest love and compassionate relation", "go and manifest wealth", "go and manifest happiness and success etc". But I do not suggest these things just after the moment you ask me how to use this law. The Law of Attraction is always working, even when you are upset, unfocussed, and full of negative energy.

So, my ways or mantras to use the law of attraction have 5 steps which should be followed in the order I state, and I am very sure that you'll end up being happy and content.

STEP 1: FOCUS ON HEALING

To start with the manifestation process, we need to release ourselves from all the baggage and wounds we have been carrying from past lives and all the karmic leftovers we have, and this is a very necessary thing. Take the instance of a hot air balloon, it cannot fly up in the sky until we release the basket and similarly you have to do it with yourself.

Starting to heal starts from being aware, when you become conscious about your wound then 80% of the work is already done. And then all you have to do is trust yourself and believe that these wounds and this pain will heal itself.

A strong intention requires inner strength. Many desires reside in a place where you aren't currently at, and you have to keep your thoughts, words, and actions positive and in alignment with your intention to ultimately attract your desire. You know that your intention is for your best interest, but as you set your intention, there will be a temptation to fall back into the old habits and patterns that ultimately keep you from what you want to attract. The light energy wants you, but so does the dark.

Also, you might think a healthy lifestyle has nothing to do with a positive mind, but it does. Foods are chemicals that affect the way we think. Eat foods that support health, give energy, and promote a positive outlook on life. These are vegetables, legumes, whole grains, fruits, etc. You know what the right diet is. Exercise. You need a fit body so you can keep going and also enjoy the journey.

STEP 2: COME INTO HEART

Giving your heart the lead in this whole process is what I suggest. The heart is the seat of the soul, and it is basically a connection between you and your higher self, and I'll be mentioning a few more reasons why should we let the heart rule later.

But for now, envisioning from your heart is more suggested because that leads to much faster results and you mostly manifest according to your soul's wants and desires. The heart leads and mind follow. As in the end, we have to achieve balance through the combined conscious states of the heart and mind.

Self-limiting thoughts seep into your mind consciously and unconsciously. At your lowest, you may think you don't deserve the universe's blessings. Even when you feel you are prepared to accept a blessing; your unconscious mind may sabotage your success by quietly telling you that you aren't worthy of that, or blessing won't be enough. To stop these self-limiting thoughts, you need to clear your mind before making an intention. Simply put, if you don't believe you deserve what you're seeking, you're not going to get it. Those deep, subconscious fears and doubts send messages loud and clear too. If part of you feels as though you don't deserve what you're seeking, then that part of you is competing with your desire.

Allow each day to be filled with hope, belief, strength, and passion for what is to come—release doubt, worry, and fear. Keep your actions aligned with your intentions and your desires will naturally attract. Negative emotion does not serve you. It is an illusion to hold you back. Potential mistakes and challenges can arise and that's okay—that's part of the fun of it. You always learn something new and grow just a little more.

STEP 3: FOCUS ON PRESENT

The future is a succession of "todays". In this concept, it is very important that we feel this moment, that we realize how precious this moment could be. All you need to do is FEEL GOOD NOW! Eventually, when you will cultivate this feeling and generate emotions towards it then you will start feeling the content within yourself.

Once you start living the present and you sense the peace, the beauty, the joy this moment has for you then gradually you will notice that you enjoy this presentation and you do not wish to materialize things anymore. So, does something which brings out your passion or something which makes you focus on the present? Consciously working the Law of Attraction to your advantage can bring you success beyond what you may have previously thought impossible. The potential for everything exists in God and the Universe, but the ability to attract exists in you. Every day, continue to receive and feel the positive energy and emotions flow through, so you can live in a state of constant allowing and receiving for your highest good. A state of continual success.

I find that focusing on manifesting is limited and exhausting since it leaves God out. It often involves a shopping list of what the ego wants to "get from the universe." By its very nature that's profoundly limited.

STEP 4: RELEASE THE OUTCOME

Now is the time when I will be opposing everything that you have heard about how to practice the law of attraction. People will tell you to send out a message to the universe and you will have it materialized but I do it the other way round.

I prefer you to go with the flow and trust what destiny has for you. See how life unfolds its path to you and what all beautiful surprises it has to offer. This step is interlinked to the previous one as it forces you to be present in this moment. In this step, you go with one affirmation, and it goes as, "I MAY MANIFEST THE HIGHEST OUTCOME POSSIBLE!" and this is where the whole perception changes.

You ask the universe to give rather than telling the universe what to give. Here you can go by showing your abundance and this comes when you start with being more grateful. So, you can go every day like "thank you for the warm shower", "thank you for a nice sleep" or "thank you that I am not late for work today" and so on.

The Universe rarely delivers all that you desire in one fell swoop, but rather gives you bits and pieces of the puzzle to realize and put together. For each bit and piece, you must trust that it is being delivered for your best interest overall and be thankful for it. Thankfulness for what you already have before your desires are delivered is the main ingredient in this recipe for success.

STEP 5: LET LIFE TAKE THE LEAD

You may not sometimes know what exactly you want, and you do not get any guidance from within, nor do you know what is going to happen. Hence, this is the time when you should leave everything on destiny, and you should trust life. The effectiveness of your belief systems is built on a foundation of trust. What you feel is true can only be true for you if you trust that your belief process will ultimately bring your desires to fruition. If you feel that your beliefs will not attract your best life, you do not trust them, and they will not help attract what you seek, but something else.

A beautiful way of manifestation is to surrender you and to leave everything on the universe and soul. I mean is there any fun of life if you know what problems you will face?—No, right! You can often ask for signs (will be discussing them later) and affirm the universe that it can intervene in your path. All this surrendering does is that it takes the baggage off your shoulder. All the tensions and problems you carry just keep on weighing up and leaving everything on the universe and that divine power just reduces a bit of that weight.

MANIFESTATION SKILLS

Now you know how to use the law of attraction what next? Google how to implement them? HEH! I am very sure you will be answered by start thinking about good things and you should sit and daydream about your desires, make manifestation boards, etc, etc. But you know what if you manifest like this, it'll be very slow and you may not get the results and you will ask "why can't I manifest?" because obviously, we need everything in a short span. I've heard it lamented over, and over again, "I don't get it! I've been so positive since I've learned about the law of attraction. Why is all this bad stuff suddenly happening to me? I better stop all this wishful thinking. I've got REAL problems to deal with!"

The reason behind this big flaw is that your subconscious mind is much more powerful than your conscious mind. And if you go for a mind-centered manifestation instead of a heart-centered one then you will surely face very despair and remain unsatisfied. Your mind carries a whole in a world full of problems, wounds, and pains, the baggage of past lives and karma, and whatnot. You have to synchronize your mind with your heart. Let the heart lead and mind follow.

Well I know you must be very curious to know how to make the law of attraction work, the question arises is where to implement? How to manifest?

KNOCK KNOCK! Do not worry, I am still here!

Living in today's time and fast forward world we all are eager to know how we can manifest our dreams, but before I tell you all the secrets there is this million-dollar question which is how do you know what dreams to manifest and what not?

Well, well, while moving forward I would like to tell you that there are two types of dreams. There are TYPES of dreams?—Yes, indeed!

We remember only a fraction of our dreams on any night – if and when we do. These dream fragments fade from memory as the day progresses. This is the case with ordinary dreams or EGO dreams. Yet there is another category of the dream that is not so forgettable and that is the vivid, profound, or spiritual dream or SOUL dreams.

Ego dreams are nothing but a vision of our desires or wants. They are an emotional release of whatever feelings we suppressed all through the day due to some societal pressure or any other reason. We generally see ordinary dreams and try to manifest them.

What happens is that our mind or ego carries a suitcase of all the wounds and pain and all the trash, so when we let our ego talk, we just start to ruin things ourselves. When we try to manifest ego dreams we do not feel complete or content or happy. We do not feel peace or success and the reason is, we are not in alignment with our soul, we are not guided by the soul which makes us feel so empty and lonely.

Whereas, in soul dreams, it is the message of the soul, the higher self, you have to distinguish between these two types. And we should try to manifest soul dreams and not ego dreams. You may ask why? The reason being that it is an ego dream clarifies most of the question. Take an example of an ego dream where you see someone whom you love or a person you want to pursue, you may start manifesting this vision and then you may pursue that person also, you both may have a great relation ahead but then moving forward in life you will notice that the relation starts to fall apart, or you do not feel complete and in a moment. And trust me; I have been a victim of this situation. That is why ego dreams should not be manifested.

Okay, no ego dreams, but how to distinguish between these dreams? Well when you see a soul vision, these dreams don't evaporate from your memory over the day. They are visually more vivid and have a richer atmosphere where the dreamer seems to be in a state of heightened awareness. One of the hallmarks of the visionary dream is the richness of meaning. Often the meaning of the images in these dreams is multi-layered and the dreamer has the pleasure of experiencing 'light bulb' moments as the meaning unpacks itself due to some external trigger in waking life that occurs soon after the dream and then weeks, months and even years later.

You are moved to pleasure by visions of ineffable beauty which you have never beheld in the physical world. In dreams, we catch glimpses of a life larger than our own. Thoughts are imparted to us far above our ordinary thinking.

When you manifest these soul dreams, the happiness and contentment, and the degree of guidance you get are just so high up in the sky. Although it takes time for them to mix in your awareness, the clearness of the dream may force you to question if that was your soul dream!

We are actively working to create our dreams, and the Universe is aligning to deliver them to us. Below is my four-step formula to manifest your soul dreams and desires so that your mind and soul are in sync.

STEP 1: UNDERSTAND WHAT YOU NEED

The very basic to this process is to know what you want and

what your soul wishes for you in this lifetime. You will have to drop all your conditioning and cravings and let the universe intervene.

As an example, suppose a person is an engineer but he loves dancing, he took this profession due to family pressure or say you do not earn much as a dancer, so he pursued engineering. Hence, if he sees any dance show auditions while watching TV and skips it that would be careless of him or ignorant of him.

Whereas if he lets his passion make the move and connects to his talents then he would be able to manifest his desires easily because when he does this, he is following what natural gifts and talents he has.

To really work with the Law of Attraction, be intentional with your thoughts, feelings, and actions. Intention focuses your brain activity and uses every available resource to help you perform an action. This type of disciplined focus will help you achieve faster and more accurate results when using the Law of Attraction. Act and say as if you have already achieved that.

STEP 2: ASK UNIVERSE TO REVEAL SOUL'S DREAMS

There will be numerous times when your soul would not reveal everything in one single dream, or you would see some things and activities in your dream, but you cannot decipher how it should be done or what exactly it asks you to do. Hence, it is very important to trust your soul and heart.

The key to recognizing most soul dreams is a simple question: "Does it feel familiar?" Did you already know that expect that, feel that, or think that? The familiarity of the dream's story or concept is often a clue to its source. Not always, but often. You can also test the dream's fruit. A dream from God will produce good fruit in your life, while a dream filled with earthly wisdom will produce bad fruit

You can use affirmations like" I don't know what my soul

dreams are right now, so I am willing to let go of what I think my soul dreams are to welcome my soul's desires" and this surrendered lifestyle helps you to manifest more efficiently. As long as you do your daily mind-clearing practices, you will be guided towards your goals.

You need to switch from "I WANT FROM LIFE" to "WHAT LIFE WANTS FROM ME". It is a very healthy and happy way to live and manifest. As you practice this, notice an excitement building up in your spirit. You feel encouraged & inspired.

STEP 3: FOLLOW THROUGH WITH ACTION

Now when you start getting what your soul and universe want from you, it is time to prepare yourself to receive signals in consciousness too.

These signs need not be very big or dramatic, can be very normal and negotiable but that's the whole new challenge, right? Therefore, it is necessary here to follow your intuitions and your soul.

You need to visualize your dreams and a very good trick to visualize them is to do before you sleep. Focus on the sensations and feelings and make them as real as possible. Also, when it comes to manifesting your dreams, you need to meet the Universe halfway by moving towards them. Mindfulness is the practice of self-awareness without judgment. When you are mindful, you aren't just aware of what you're feeling and thinking, you're observing it without analyzing it. Don't take any action without first announcing your intention to take that action. Again, it feels tedious at first, but soon, you'll notice something incredible:

The simple act of washing a dish is really a series of several actions, movements, and thoughts. And when your intention is focused on the action, you'll appreciate exactly how much movement is involved.

Affirmations work wonderfully for many people who start out

with the Law of Attraction. And there are plenty of Law of Attraction affirmations that you can try out for yourself. Use affirmations with feelings. Write a list of empowering beliefs that you want to have, such as I am enough. I am powerful. I am loved. I am financially secure. And make sure you feel them as you say them. The feeling is the secret ingredient.

STEP 4: RINSE + REPEAT

This is the toughest step indeed. You have to rinse your energy felid every time you start manifesting. The three main ingredients to this whole 4-step formula are patience, consistency, and openness.

Patience is needed to wait for the signs to come and wait for the soul to reveal the whole path for this lifespan. Consistency is needed because this is not some magic, it is a very long process, and you just cannot manifest by following this once. And last but not least is openness, and it plays the key role here because only if you learn and are open to new things and surprises, then only you can see the signs in the conscious state. If you learn to be happy now, learn to be abundant now then most of the manifestation is already done.

Sometimes you will be thrown challenges or things that appear "bad" at first. But later, you will discover that they helped you to evolve and find true joy. Other times, you will experience "good" things which may turn out to harm you, which may later help you to grow stronger. Can you see how nothing is linear? Everything is connected and is perfectly orchestrated. There's no need to worry.

Addressing your fears and doubts is important. But after a brief acknowledgment, replace those fears and doubts with appreciation and gratitude. These new, positive feelings change your perspective and expectations, opening up to the possibility that more great things are on your horizon. Feel grateful and appreciative of how this law has already worked so well for you.

Make a list of all the great things in your life and express your appreciation for those things. Expressing gratitude is the key to setting yourself up for more and better things. As you move further with reading you will know how being grateful to small things can change your life.

UNRAVEL THE TRUTHS

While acquiring all this knowledge about the law of attraction, unlike everyone I do not want to keep you in any false mind state, but debates are going on all over the world and among spiritual circles about this law, and there are certain truths and facts about this law which are rarely discussed. Everything has free will in this universe. In other words, your thoughts should have free will to be manifested. You can be skilled in the Law of Attraction and attract whatever you wish for, but if it interferes with somebody's free will, it will not provide you well and can wish ill upon you. To be honest you are also fighting with other people's desires—both good and bad. So, be aware that if your desire is in direct rivalry with someone else's stronger desire, the universe will answer accordingly. The Law of Attraction does not give you full and total control of your life, it only states that like will attract like. And you can use this to your advantage by being willful with your desires, but this isn't a piece of cake. So, before you start manifesting blindly do read these truths once.

TRUTH 1: IT ISNT ALL ABOUT THOUGHTS

When we say 'materialize your thoughts' we forget the part that heart also plays a role in this. Your energy field or electromagnetic field, the aura is the non-physical shell or layer of energy that surrounds and interpenetrates the physical body. The aura and the specific fields of various organs such as the heart have been scientifically measured. And that is why I call our energy field as a Quantum Communication Device. The heart has the capacity to dial a call to the universe.

The heart and the mind are what I call powerhouses of this field. Do you remember I said to reveal more reasons for why you should manifest by heart and not brain? Here is the reason-The heart is the most powerful generator of electromagnetic energy in the human body, producing the largest rhythmic electromagnetic field of any of the body's organs. The heart's electrical field is about 60 times greater in amplitude than the electrical activity generated by the brain. Therefore, your heart is a stronger and pure manifester than your brain.

While our thoughts do tend to create our reality, they are not solely responsible for situations in our lives. If our thinking was always 100% responsible for our reality, then we would always get precisely what we want when we want it and we would be heading a satisfying life. The fact is that our thoughts aren't solely responsible for our reality. Our vibration doesn't always attract experiences that "match it." Otherwise, benevolent people wouldn't die horrible deaths, and cruel people wouldn't live fantastic lives.

TRUTH 2: THIS IS NOT THE ONLY LAW

The cosmos we have is a very enormous thing. It is such a complex mechanism up there! The Law of Attraction is not the only law we have in this universe there and end number of things which aren't even discovered yet.

Just think, if one single law has been discussed so much then what would have happened if we knew about many other laws as well? We do not even know about laws like, the Law of Contagion is a magical law which suggests that once two people or objects have been in contact a magical link persists between them unless or until a formal cleansing, consecration, exorcism, or other act of banishing breaks the non-material bond.

Or let us take another law, the Law of Gender. It has very little to do with biological sex. Rather, it refers to the fact that there are two major types of energy. You can think of them as masculine and feminine, as yin and yang, or as anima and animus. We all contain a certain amount of both energy and must find a way to achieve a balance between both types if we are to live authentically and happily.

The actuality is that Law of attraction only governs reality and that is why we focus on this. It is just believed by many to be a universal law by which "Like Always Attracts like." The results of positive thoughts are always positive consequences.

TRUTH 3: IT DOES NOT CAUSE BAD THINGS

People are often found blaming the law of attraction for a breakup, or loss of someone or if something bad happen. And in return, their mind says, "You only attracted this!"

I mean come on; I am sick of hearing this conversation; no one ever attracts bad to them. No one ever wishes to have bad. And if it would be so then why do not we blame the law of attraction for a rape? Why don't we blame it for a car accident? There should be no need for police officers if the law of attraction is responsible for everything. We do not because we know that everything isn't like this, everything is not in your power, and they are destined to be so.

We start believing that people who lose their children to suicide or develop cancer do so because "their vibration is manifesting these events" or "their thoughts are attracting their reality" However, not only are these beliefs are insanely simplistic and short-sighted, but they also express an unspoken lack of empathy towards others.

Let me make an understanding of this point. Link TRUTH 1 to this, the higher the energy, lighter experiences, and the lower the energy, the denser the experience. Here lighter experiences mean the feeling of peace, joy, love, and compassion, and all the bliss and denser experiences mean more intense and dark feelings and instances. But this again does not mean that everything would be bliss for a high energy field person, and everything just sucks up for a low energy person.

TRUTH 4: DIVINE TIMING IS STRONGER

The meaning of divine timing is that it is the belief that everything that happens in your life occurs at precisely the right moment. The universe is here to take care of you and will never put you in a place that you can't handle.

Patience is perhaps the hardest and the most important rule to embrace when it comes to divine timing. It can be difficult to accept that the universe will give you what you want when you need it, and patience can be elusive. If you do feel impatient, really examine that emotion.

You can also look at divine timing as the way the universe manifests your dreams and goals in its way. You may manifest to be a leading actor in a certain film, but you didn't get that, whereas what happens after some time is that you get a movie bigger than the previous one.—DING! DING!

So, let the divine and ultimate power make the decisions for you. Nothing is manifested without the will of God or your destiny. Nothing will come into your life even a minute before it is manifested to be. Thereby, LET GO AND LET GOD. When we cling to the past or the way things used to be, we have a challenging time accepting universal timing. Try to let go of what once was and embrace what could be because that's where divine timing lives.

At the end of this chapter, a little tip is what I will leave. DO NOT TRY TO STOP THE FLOW. As a motivational speaker and a manifester I will always suggest you to never try and change your destiny or regret that you could have changed it because, no, you cannot change it plus I am damn sure you will lead a beautiful life once you start accepting and keep your heart open.

Many conclude that these "concepts" seem too outlandish to apply across the board. Fear, worry, and doubt seem more reasonable. They hit a wall. This wall is your weak spot! When the infatuation ends, you will begin to see whether you have faith. You will start to become aware of how much power you are consciously using, with mere glimpses of the staggering power which is available to you!

Also, before leaving I would like to leave a curiosity, the Law of Attraction bridge you with higher and spiritual planes of existence, when you start practicing these methods, you begin to see beyond the normal and this not so extraordinary world. A strange and bigger, brighter world opens up to you which is brimming with possibility. Now keep thinking about this new brighter world until I breakthrough your curiosity!

PART II

KNOW YOUR COMRADES

When darkness is all around me

And life is hard to bear

I know HE will send a part of me

So that I conquer all what I prayer

That part of me shall not remain with me forever

But it is certain that they make me clever

This sense of love is so overwhelming

But it's not always necessary that it has a beautiful ending.

~ *Priyal Bansal*

ANGLES AND COMPANIONS

Have you ever come across a person who you feel as though you've known "forever," even if you've just met them? Have you ever met a person who you immediately connect with, without knowing why? Have you ever felt that someone is around you, but you cannot see them? Or you feel the divine presence around you when you pass through some accident?

Well, let me tell you that yes, you have a big circle of companions and angels around you who were destined to be a part of your life even before you were born.

In this area, you will know about all these people who are connected to your soul and their purpose is to be with you and vice versa. So, you have Guardian angels, soul mates, soul group, twin flames, soul animals, kindred spirits, etc. and if you are wondering who the heck are they all? Then do not worry, they are just some entities and spiritual mates for you in this lifetime.

They are part of us, and we are part of them, we are never actually alone. The reason our world is full of spirit guides is to protect and support us on our paths and journeys. Spiritual Accompaniment, also known as Spiritual Direction, is a process to help you come closer to God. Through conversation with a spiritual companion in an atmosphere of trust, you can be helped to arrive at a deeper awareness of the presence and movement of God in your everyday life. As you share your dreams, struggles, triumphs, and fears, you open up to the deepest and wisest source of freedom and joy. A spiritual companion helps you notice, savour, and respond to the movement of God in the spiritual practice of ordinary life. The companion is a listening and supportive person who creates an environment where you can look honestly at your relationship with God. When we are working on our purpose, they show up for us in full force to help carry out the purpose we were assigned to complete. Each reunion unfolds like a perfect treasure map that gives its seekers goose bumps! The treasure, though extremely hard-won, is what these seekers have always dreamed of and never thought they would hold—undying.

GUARDIAN ANGELS

Have you ever heard to be in the angelic realm? Or about your fairy godmother? In the following part, I am going to bridge your understanding and actuality about angels.

Starting with what the internet defines a guardian angel, we get "an angel that is assigned to protect and guide a particular person, group, kingdom, or country". But for me, my angels are everything. When I started my spiritual journey, I felt so blessed to know about them and to know how much they adore me.

Angels are celestial messengers that move at the speed of light to carry out God's will. They are anxious to hear and carry out God's Word. Their inexhaustible love for God motivates them to protect and guard what is most precious to Him, His children. In this journey of life, man has uncountable dangers to pass through, and hence to his protection, allmighty sends his angels with you.

Knowing of this belief, you may ask that, is protecting us the only purpose of angels? Alleluia, they are not just here to protect you but also to guide you, to pray for you, to record your deeds, and help you throughout whether you thank them or not.

Your angels may be praying to God for you so that he makes you struggle less. Buddhism believes that these angels watch over people, listen to people's prayers, and join in with the good thoughts that people pray. God's gift of the Holy Spirit enables us to speak to our Heavenly Father from the depths of our hearts.

People of many faiths believe that guardian angels record everything that people think, say, and do in their lifetimes and then pass the information along to higher-ranking angels to include in the universe's official records. And this can be linked to what we say Karma. Every person will be judged according to their words and their deeds, whether good or evil.

I am sure you must be overwhelmed after reading this. After all angels are so caring just like our mothers. Don't you want to connect to them? Don't you want to thank them and communicate with them? And what if they are sending you signal?

Well, well, it is very easy to contact them. They are waiting for you to call out them so that they can show love and affection to you more prominently. But yes, there are certain methods from my experience which are completely reliable to contact and thank your angels.

METHOD 1: PRESENT GRATITUDE

So, this one is a very helpful way to not just contact angels but also as I mentioned previously to manifest better. My teacher who helped me explore this subject, made me start this practice. And all you have to do here is make a gratitude journal, and start thanking for 10 things per day. I started very basic like "thank you, angels, for giving me a pen", "thank you, angels, for giving me a family" etc. But then within a week or so I felt something very good and positive around me and that feeling persists.

And yes, fix a place where you write this journal, it could be a garden, your balcony, or your room, where ever you feel relaxed.

METHOD 2: HOW THEY LOOK

Moving forward with my journey, as I grew eager and wanted to know how to connect to them, my teacher told me that imagine how you want your angel to be. Design or customize an angel for yourself. Whether you want it to be male or female, you want it to have big wings or not, you want it to be a typical fairy or some person/ancestor/relative and this customization goes on. Believe me on this, by personifying your angels; it is easy for them to appear to you because you have asked them to appear that way. Hence you will know the exact moment even in consciousness when your angel appears.

METHOD 3: SET A TIME

Okay so, set some time to talk to them, as we do to meet someone, similarly do it with your angels, and decide someplace where you can detach yourself from this physical world. This place can be where you write your gratitude journal, or it can in the morning at your bed when you wake up, can be a place in the home where you worship, it can be anywhere. All you need to have is the feeling of excitement or joy; I mean this feeling cannot be described in words. Your angels would be already present there even before you because as I stated, they want to talk to you, but they cannot until you want them to.

METHOD 4: MEDITATION

When you meditate, again, choose a place where you see fit to enter your higher consciousness. While meditating focus on your heart being the seat of your soul, focus on depth, and then gradually come to the middle. Slowly and steadily pass this focus to the center of your head and then when you can see white light widening around, pass this focus to the angelic realm. It can be called the halfway, where you see your angels. Call out for them," Angels please appear to me" and try to focus on the image you created of how you wanted your angel to be. BOOM! What do you see? The same figure personified.

But I will leave a side note over here that you won't experience this the very first day, you have to practice this and follow your intuitions.

METHOD 5: ASK FOR SIGNS

Now when we are through with all the imagining and gratitude, ask you angels to show their presence in symbols. As for me, I started with a feather, I said to them to show me a feather as I imagined it and prove to me that you are near me. Trust me on this, I was having my afternoon meal and I saw a bunch of those feathers on my sleeve, and I was jumping around! And I went to tell my teacher about this, she said now when it is proved to you that your angels are around you and you have established a connection, just ask them anything. So, I went back and started asking those questions in situations I was confused about and told them to answer through some symbols, and that is how I started getting messages.

So just ask for their presence, and it could be through any number or any animal, some colour, etc. but just do not push yourself too hard and be in that search 24/7.

Sometimes it's hard to believe God could be that active or bring that love to our life. Truth is—He is. God is awesome like that. We need to remind ourselves of just what an awesome gift from God our guardian angel is—a gift that, too often, goes untapped. Many of us are taught about angels neither from the Bible nor from meditations of the Saints, but from media. Everything cannot be believed with closed eyes. What the world has to offer you has some truths also. The same is with the concept of angels, everything that spiritual teachers tell you about them is true, but they do not tell the less known truths. So here are some truths about angels.

TRUTH 1: IT IS A GROUP

We are generally conditioned to believe that only one angel is assigned to you for this lifetime, but the truth is every angel has a purpose to serve. If you are going through financial crises then you have a different angel, you have a different angel to help you pass through a dark phase, I had a different angel while writing the book, and you have a different angel while reading the book. So, this is not at all important that you have a single angel after you.

TRUTH 2: THEY CHOOSE YOU

People often think that by calling out an angel they choose them, or they get whoever angel was free but the truth here is that even before you are born or put in your mother's womb, angels chose to protect and guide you. They willingly pray god to assign them your protection and that is the reason they are with you throughout because they prayed solemnly before god to have you.

TRUTH 3: ANGELS ARE NOT HUMANS

As a child, we are often told after a loved one's death that they will become an angel, but the truth is that neither angels were ever humans nor humans can ever be angels. While there is some debate about when exactly angels were created, but we know for sure that angels came before humans and most likely before the earth as well. One thing we can be certain about is that the angels were created before the seventh day of creation. The Bible says: "Thus the heavens and the earth were completed, and all their hosts" (Genesis 2:1).

TRUTH 4: THEY ARE SENSITIVE

I always wondered why I do not connect with my angels when I feel sad, angry, or egoist? But only until I didn't know about this truth. Angels are highly sensitive and even they feel emotions and pain more than we do. They have hearts just as we do, and it hurts them more than us when we go through pain. And they distance themselves from us when we emit negative emotions and vibes because they can only handle this up to a limit. They maintain a distance when they cannot take more pain. And did you just link this to why we need to stay positive? Boom, you were right!

TRUTH 5: THEY ARE FASTEST

Do you consider light to be traveling the fastest? Well, good morning, angels are even faster. They are not possessed of any material body as we are and soon as we ask them to help someone or do something even at a distanced place, they will do and come back to you even before you realize. I have experienced this multiple times. Once someone was sharing their experience with angels and told that they had to go for a meeting and just before the meeting was about to start, they had a call from family telling that their father needs to be hospitalized. And the person just closed their eyes and said their angels to go and give their father all the strength they need and trust me, when the person went to the hospital, the family was just signing father's discharge papers. I know this makes you go like "Awww!"

So, believe in your angels and trust that whatever is happening will for sure bring happiness at the end.

No one dies unhappy.

SOUL MATES

What definition clicks you when you think of this word? Romantic partner? Lifelong relation? Strongest bond? DING DING! This is not what we are talking about. Although today's soul mate is referred to a romantic partner with the implication of an exclusive lifelong bond. It commonly holds the connotation of being the strongest bond with another person that one can achieve. But it isn't all about this; they are much more than a romantic partner and an unbreakable bond.

Spiritually speaking, a soul mate is a friend of your soul which you have for this lifespan because they help in your development. When we meet a soul mate we are all joined in an ancient and eternal union with humanity that cuts across all barriers of time, convention, philosophy, and definition.

And to your surprise, we have more than one soul mate. Yes, and because it is not about all love in the air, soul mates can be a part of your family, your friend circle, someone on the other side of the world but for sure you have more than one soul mate. When we meet our soul mate, pretty much they are very equal spiritually. However, from experience they hold something different for everyone.

A Soul Mate is a member of your soul family. When we meet them, the frequency of our energy and their energy resonates, you connect as if you are known to them from a past life. Soul Mates serve as mirrors of us. What we see in another soul reflects our soul. A soul mate's purpose is to shake you up, tear apart your ego a little bit, break your heart open so new light can get in.

Now, many people generally fall in our best friend or close friend category throughout our life. There will be many who will be categorized as a special friend too. It is easy to name these people as soul mates or just friends but what about those who tend to be best friends but do not click at a romantic level? More than a friend but not your boyfriend/ girlfriend?

Well, these are the relations about which you will be known as you go through the rest of the pages. So basically, we have four soul mate connections and each one serves as a mirror. What we see in another soul reflects our soul.

There comes a mysterious meeting in life when someone acknowledges who we are and what we can be, igniting the circuits of our highest potential. Relationships with soul mate potential come around a lot more often than you might imagine. The problem is, we're not always available for them.

Let's find out what the spiritual connection between these different types of relationships are, what all types of soul mates you have, and what their purpose in your life is.

SOUL TEACHER

Do you have someone who teaches you something every day? Maybe not intentionally but unknowingly?

Well, soul teacher is a person who appears in our lives to help teach us vital life lessons. Sometimes these lessons are taught deliberately, and other times these lessons are unintentional. A Soul Teacher is someone who helps our soul grow and evolve during its time on Earth. These are the people who seemingly push our buttons and make us angry, upset, sad, and a whole myriad of emotions that sometimes overwhelm us.

My soul teacher is my tuition teacher, and I am so grateful to her that she opened these spiritual gates to me, she challenged and supported me to think and experience broadly. These people see the potential in you and push you towards the extremes. On a positive note, these are the people who challenge our thinking and help us widen our perspective. These are the people who teach us how to love unconditionally and to forgive. These are also the people who encourage us and help us bring out our talents and potential.

My teacher taught me to be positive throughout, to be kind and helpful to everyone, she taught me to keep my inner child awaken always and never let that innocence go off you. Soul mate teachers are very special, sacred relationships and each of us has been in both roles—student and teacher—whether we realized it at the time or not.

What signs should you be counting on when you feel this acquaintance? In my experience, you can tell that you've found your teacher when you feel an immediate strong and intense link of love for their teachings. No matter how much they scream at you or how much you dislike them, deep down you cannot accept the fact that you don't love them.

Still, the most common signs to confirm whether the person is your soul teacher or not, they must have travelled the mystic path himself to be able to show the way, must have become refined and educated to be an educator, must be generous and devoid of self-importance so that they can sacrifice wealth on behalf of the disciple and the most important is that they will not abandon you for the sake of the world. And I feel so immensely blessed to have experienced all of these signs.

Teachers are genuine vehicles of Spirit that contribute toward our collective evolution. Unlike other teachers, spiritual guides are faced with the most difficult teaching of all: to teach others the way of ego death and surrender into divine truth. Ultimately, the teacher is a ferryman who takes you from the shores of your ego to the shores of Divine Union.

SOUL COMPANION

Remember the definition of soul mates we perceive now? Yes, this would come the closest to that. Soul companions are necessary nourishment. Just like the human body needs food and water, the soul requires companion soul mates. This is the most common spiritual soul mate connection; these relationships tend to be the most harmonious and pleasing.

In terms of romance, this relationship is great to be in, with great energy you can live happily for a long time. Many times, the relationships you develop with these people will feel as though you've known them for centuries, even from past lives. With a Soul Companion, there is a great and deep understanding of the other person and a feeling that you are both on the same 'wavelength' of thoughts and emotions. One of the reasons for such depth and harmony is because they usually share with us the same Soul Age (different levels of advancement a soul obtains throughout its reincarnation journey is soul age).

In my experience, we had such an obsessive relation and we used to be the "relationship goals" amongst our friends but due to some circumstances the relationship fell apart, still, there was something which kept us together for years in contact. Soul Companions experience soulful harmony with us. The nature of a Soul Companion is much more long-lived and stable.

But we often fall into relations who give us such mystical feelings; you may start considering them as your companions and keep yourself in a false dilemma. Therefore, the signs you should focus on are that you accept them without thinking, there is a deep and unspoken respect between both of you, your instincts have kicked in to feel as if this person is your mate, both of you know what the other one will speak next. The conversation never gets old between the two of you. And most importantly a person you can let go gracefully.

If you find out whether the person is your soul companion, do not confront it to them, let them come and tell you that they want to be with you forever.

Moving ahead, I don't like to keep you in your "la-la land", sorry but I have to break that bubble. There are certain truths about soul companions that will for sure make it easier for you to find them.

TRUTH 1: THEY MAY NOT STAY FOREVER

I guess you must have summarized soul companions with the notion of "always and forever", but the truth is that sometimes they stay for a season and sometimes for a lifetime. Their purpose may just be to teach us a lesson or to help us cope with something in life.

TRUTH 2: THESE RELATIONS NEED WORK

A very popular myth about soul mates is that they do not need effort. We believe that fact of knowing them from past lives wholeheartedly. Whereas the thing is, these relations also need nurturing; they also require time, effort, patience, and diligence like any other relationship. In my case, initially, there were hundreds of trust tests; we needed to support each other. That proved to us, even these relations will fail if we do not keep conscious maintenance.

TRUTH 3: THEY DO NOT COMPLETE US

We generally, even in spiritual circles take soul companions as someone who is our better halves. No, they are not. They are helpers and catalysts in our spiritual growth. And the reason why this belief is so popular is that it gives us a reason to bypass our responsibilities and happiness. So many people enter relationships believing their soul mate will give them everything they need. This, unfortunately, leads to issues such as co-dependency, toxic enabling, and self-betrayal.

SOUL FRIEND

If you have seen the Harry Potter series, then this won't be so tough for you to understand. The trio of Harry, Hermione, and Ron is a perfect example of how soul friends work. They symbolize the promise of eternal friendship.

This is the most common type of soul mate connection. These are peopling who vibe with you the most. Soul friends are more essence-based. In other words, soul friends share our deepest dreams, values, and drives, not just similar personalities, and tastes. These are the people in your life who you have chosen because your ego, intelligence, or emotions are harmonious with the others. Essentially, you share the same tastes, interests, beliefs, sense of humour, and values.

While this connection is not as deep as a Soul Companion, a Soul Friend's company creates little friction. Sometimes Soul Friends can become Soul Teachers, but generally, you are the one who chooses your Soul Friend as you perceive the world in a similar way to them.

More than ever the importance of making and learning how to be a true soul friend is a vital part of life satisfaction in our increasingly disconnected society. The reality is that our perceptions of "friendship" have weakened so much that most of us struggle to even identify our mutual close friends. So how can we find our soul friend?

For me, a man's growth is seen in the successive choirs of his friends and there is nothing shameful as to distrust them than to be deceived by them. A soul friend will be someone with whom you can talk about anything, there is no walking on eggshells, their criticism will be constructive to you, and you truly feel understood and heard in their presence. They see your boundaries; they value your perceptions and see the best in you.

A true soul friend is with you through your darkest nights and brightest days. As loyal, compassionate companions they are by your side when you are at your absolute worst, offering a helping hand and shoulder to lean on for support—and also when you're at your most happy and successful, cheering you on in the sidelines. Regardless of what point you're at in life, soul friends are the most loyal companions, confidants, and comforters.

SOUL TWIN

Your best friends may fall into this category. Finding our Soul Twin often feels like finding a piece of ourselves that was missing. The ancient Greeks believed that our souls were once whole and the Gods divided them into two different halves, and once we found our other halves we would become whole and complete again. That is the essence of Soul Twins.

The Soul Twins assist you in releasing stagnant energy and patterns that consciously or unconsciously get held in our energy bodies. When you can re-establish your energy flow and connection to your true self and all that is, you can be limitless.

When we meet our Soul Twin we feel as though we have finally "found our home" because Soul Twins are a source of unconditional love in our lives that mirror precisely what we need to find, which is wholeness within ourselves. This love can be grounded in unconditional affection that requires significant spiritual development to first overcome the fears and possessive attachments that are involved in most typical relationships.

If you have met your Soul Twin your relationship may be intense, or it may be harmonious. Once the process of spiritual alchemy has been accepted, Soul Twins undergo a process of spiritual purification together as each side surrenders the old and invites the new. While Soul Twin relationships can be overwhelming and intimidating, they help us to ripen and mature into our fullest potential reminding us that we are children of Divinity.

They also experience immense levels of comfort with each other that cannot be experienced in other relationships, and they complement each other in many ways through their strengths and weaknesses.

Towards the conclusion, you may or may not have the capacity to find your soul mate but if your intuitions overpower these doubts then keep your heart open to all the upcoming situations and surprises. Finally, don't overlook the possibility that you may have already found your soul mate! Remember to investigate whether your soul mate is already in your life right now, right underneath your nose!

TWIN FLAMES

Let me start with a little storyline. Imagine yourself at the top of this globe, above you are all stars and planets, and your soul is just about to go through this blue and green surface, standing next to the divine power. Guess what happens! God decides to compile similar souls, and this becomes your soul group. Now the souls formed alongside you are your soul mates, and you may meet them through your life (maybe not all but some) on this earth. But what about twin flames? They are in an actual sense of your "better half".

In Greek mythology, it is believed that man had two faces, four arms and four legs which made him immensely powerful. Thereby, the Gods decided to cut the soul into half and send them to two opposite parts of the world so that the same energy and power do not become destructive. Well, something beautiful is happening as we evolve, more people are finding their twin flames and soul mates. Isn't that amazing?

Twin flames are the most intense mirror of yourself you will have in this world. They reflect all the strengths, insecurities, weaknesses, and shadows that we possess. The purpose of the twin flame bond is to help us undergo inner work, spiritual transformation, and become the best adaptation of ourselves possible. Twin flames are born from the same egg, the same source.

If you have a twin flame, which you certainly have then you have chances that you are fated to meet this person at some point in your life journey. Both of you will be pulled together like magnets! You will know when you've connected with this person because you'll immediately experience a sense of recognition and comfort. Many people describe an uncanny sense of having known their twin flame all their lives which is normal. When you encounter the person, who carries the other half of your energy, it can create a deep and philosophical and life-altering feeling of wholeness. Remember that you only meet your twin when both of you are whole in themselves because the ultimate goal of every union is to pass through the levels of life. Though this makes a mathematical imbalance it goes like 1+1=1 rather than 1+1=2.

Twin flames are there to ignite the fires of spiritual transformation. Soul mate relationships are designed to uplift us, while the twin flame relationship is designed to challenge us. Even though you will create a joint identity, you will still keep your individuality. Twin flames know that they are comprised of two very different beings. Merging into one does not mean you forget your individual needs, wants, and dreams and you encourage that. You will find you have two identities now. Your own individual one and the one that has come about as the result of your twin flame union.

Going further down in detail it is never possible to meet your twin flame without meeting your soul mate. I first met my soul teacher and them my twin flame. I get that the feeling of curiosity; you must be extremely impatient to know other characteristics too-right? SO HERE WE GO!

1: INTENSITY

You cannot deny the attraction you feel to them even if you try to distance yourself. When you see your twin flame you see the fragment of yourself. This bond is much stronger than the soul mate connection. You feel the fireworks, you can sense the push and pull of the universe. This experience is so overwhelming.

2: PURPOSE

If you are thinking to move forward with a romantic connection with your twin flame then please STOP! Boom Boom! Your twin flame union has a purpose which is to have a great professional life. You can find your twin at the workplace or online or somewhere, but you cannot build a romantic relationship and this fact is often not told. You're both driven towards a higher spiritual/social purpose.

3: STRENGTH

As mentioned above the twin flame connection is much stronger than the soul mate connection, the strength is indestructible. You two are like a flame. And, when you meet your twin flame, the process of your evolution fastens and that is one more reason to high exertion of energy. Your strengths and weaknesses perfectly balance each other. Your twin flame is a person who you completely trust and feel a sense of inner spread around.

Twin flame love is unlike any other relationship you've ever had. It's intense and can have some very challenging phases. So, if you've met your twin, here you will learn how to master this path of sacred connection. The bond between the two is like a beast. It can't be captured. It can't be contained. It can't be tamed. Instead, it burns fiercely with an unquenchable form of intensity that is both exhilarating and formidable. Encountering each other kick-starts a dynamic new part of your life. Together you can grow to higher levels than you could separately. Whether it's on a spiritual, physical, or mental level, you support each other to go further in every aspect of your life. Life is about growth and to stagnate is not to live. Together you will find and explore opportunities for growth, being open-minded and careful to learn the valuable lessons that life throws your way.

You can help each other to heal from past wounds and hard times that happen in the present. Being loved so unconditionally is an amazing way of getting you to deal with past hurts and traumas. The continual strength, love, and support of your twin flame can get you through some of the most difficult times. It also allows you to work on emotional issues such as distrust, jealousy, and fear and completely turn them on their head.

Your twin flame could be your greatest dream or your worst nightmare. They will inflame you, test you, and love you fiercely all at once. This bond can be destructive as well as constructive. But don't get afraid! In my all-purpose book, you will find the answer to this also. So how to deal with such an intense bond? A bond that will help in your growth, inspire change, and challenge you to accept yourself fully, wholly, and solely should not be regretting?

Side note—Being a relationship adviser of my school, these tips can also be used in any relation :)

TIP 1: NO ATTACHMENT

This flame that we share with our twins is so strong and so intense that if we try to grasp on this and grow the roots of attachment, you shall see your twin flame repel this attachment. Now, to let go of attachment the very best way to do is, let go of the label. Do not label them as twin flames, soul mates, or love of your life. When you label them, you make them stand on a pedestal, and as their position rises, your expectations and attachments rise. Do not say "You are the love of my life", "I cannot live without you" etc. IT'S A BIG NO!

TIP 2: EVERYTHING IS WORKING OUT

The moment you read this; didn't you find some sort of lightness? Exactly, that's the motto! The union is so intense already, it needs no more drama. Sorry for cutting the thrill, but yes! Never over think about this relation. If you guys are talking, that's working out. If you guys fight then that is also working out. And there is no need to over think, you are one whole being yourself and you are here to grow yourself. Live with openness. A huge lesson in life is that sometimes we have to let the things we love to go for a bond to go stronger. Everything remains either for a season or for a reason.

TIP 3: YOU ARE FREE

Have you ever wondered what the sweetest thing you can say to someone is? Possibly the answer would be I LOVE YOU but no, this doesn't work that way here! In this relation, in fact, in any relationship, you need to maintain space and you need to let each other breathe this air. So, the most apt thing you say to someone is "YOU ARE FREE". Love is given in this relation; freedom is what we need to embed. Freedom and love go together. Love is not a reaction. If I love you because you love me, that is mere trade, a thing to be bought in the market; it is not loved. To love is not to ask anything in return, not even to feel that you are giving something- and it is only such love that can know freedom

Now you must interlink all the three notions. And so, shall you do, because they are. What an immense blessing. And granting all this, you both tend to mirror each other's unresolved wounds, sometimes heading to conflict; you both accept each other unconditionally. Deep down, you feel that you have known this person for eternity, and generally, you both share the same spiritual calling. You feel like a wait has ended. The direction of your life has brought you to this point and you understand why certain things had to happen the way that they did. Understanding causes all the pieces to fall into place and you'll feel more trust in both yourself and the universe.

While twin flame connections still face hardships and do not always last forever but they represent an important chance for growth and happiness. We might be heart-broken, wracked with grief, martially over-burdened, or just plain tired and disillusioned when they suddenly disappear out of the blue. But isn't that all for later? If you know you have a twin flame near you, then only you may imagine the separation. Therefore, what are the signs? Whatever emotional or psychological stage you're at in life, it is always beneficial to be conscious of the people you live with and meet. These following twin flame signs might help you to open new pathways and opportunities for the union.

1: YOU GET A SENSE OF IMPORTANCE

You have a feeling that they are going to play a very important role in your development, without knowing when, why, or how. Intuitively knowing what the other person is feeling or thinking about or doing. Plus, you find that they can detect the same things about you. You feel a strange, inexplicable sense of "recognition" when you meet the person. When you meet your Twin Flame, all skeletons come out and are eventually set free. The level of intensity experienced with your twin is unlike anything you will have experienced before. A look, a touching of hands, the sound of their voice, all evokes more emotion than you've felt before.

2: RECOGNITION

As soon as you meet this person you suddenly start vibing with each other. All you can feel is that you have known them for years more than you can count. You rack your brain trying to figure out where it may have been. You might even question each other on it. In time you realize that this recognition didn't just point to a brief prior interaction. It was recognizing someone that you've always known. You establish an immediate, intense connection with them that is invigorating and shocking at the same time. Sharing many of the same interests, values, hobbies, and preferences. For example- when I started writing this book, I told no one, but one sudden day when I thought to tell this to my twin flame, the bummer was that she was also writing a book that too on a similar topic.

3: GETTING HOME

Finding your twin feels like coming home. This is where you're meant to be and the idea of 'home' meaning a physical place or building loses meaning for you. There are no secrets and you both know each other's vulnerabilities. Feelings like you can easily communicate and discuss problems without speaking out loud. A simple look into each other's eyes will often be enough to tell you what your twin flame thinks about what's going on around. Also, I have noted that you can even share your achievements with them. They will share the same level of excitement and zeal as you. Although you might have to be away from home for a while, you'll always remember the feeling of coming back to them. I had to stay away from my twin flame; we used to have no connection for months.

4: YOU ARE BALANCED

Mirrors are a key aspect of spirituality and never more so than in the twin flame relationship. You complete each other and where you fear you fall short as individuals, together you can achieve anything. You both embody the yin and yang, in other words, your dark side is balanced by their light side, and their dark side is balanced by your light side. One aspect of your twin soul will be mirrored and balanced by you in return. If one twin is dark, the other's lightness will balance this. If one is an introverted, the other's social skills will balance this. Initially my twin flame was going through the dark night whereas I was in my bliss, so I used to give her motivation.

5: AUTHENTICITY

Feeling like it's natural and safe to be your authentic self around this person. For example, even if you are publicly shy, your twin flame will make you feel comfortable. You can be your authentic self—warts and all—without the fear of rejection, persecution, or judgment with them. Twin flames know the value of authenticity and never try to be other people. They don't stage their lives across social media or go out of their way to make others feel inferior to their connection. Far from it. They understand the gift that they have and fully embrace it. Even in the first meet, you will feel like sharing your darkest secrets.

It's quite likely that everyone has a twin flame. But not everyone can connect with their twin flame within this lifetime. Twin flames emerge within our lives when our souls are ready to undergo the process of spiritual awakening and transformation. For some people, the twin flame connection is simply too intense and is not welcomed, and hence never happens. Sometimes, our twin flames run away because the connection is too overwhelming and intense for the ego. When the ego is not ready to spiritually evolve, it resists, fights, and tries to escape—this is why twin flames run and try to avoid the relationship. Therefore remember, the main purpose is to grow and achieve goals and play your role, all the companions are just for help.

SPIRIT ANIMALS

Many people mistakenly believe that animals are inferior to humans. Since humans don't speak the same language as animals, animals and humans can't connect verbally. But see the irony, today we reach out for our pets more than our friends. Animals are beautiful creatures. They do not sow, or reap, or gather into barns, yet your heavenly Father feeds them. Aren't they more valuable than you are? And which of you by worrying can add even one hour to their life?

Let's not be cruel, they are also part of this earth, and they also have souls. You are loved by them, no matter they are loved by you or not. Animals are also messengers of God. In Indian mythology, every god and goddess is related to some of the other animals.

It was only recently that I discovered the existence of Spirit Animals. It is said that we, as human beings, possess at least one Spirit Animal in our lifetimes that serve as our protectors, guides, helpers, and companions. But usually, it is common for us to have many Spirit Animal helpers throughout different periods of our lives. If you listen and try to connect, you will find there is much to learn and experience. Connecting with your spirit animal offers understanding, harmony, and mutual respect with nature.

Going down the history lane, the concept of Spirit Animals has its origin in Animistic and Totemistic beliefs. Totemism is a system of belief which incorporates the notion that each human being has a spiritual connection to another physical being. Whereas animism has a belief that all plants, animals, and objects have spirits. And up to some level, both the believes are the same or we can say interlinked.

Those who believe in the presence of Spirit Animals not only respect the flora and fauna of the earth as equals, but they often perceive the world around them as consisting of the same universal energy. This is similar to pantheistic thought which believes that man, nature, and animal kind are all the manifestations of God.

Okay, this all seems good! But why do we need to know our spirit animals? Do they play any role in our growth? What if I fear animals? WAIT WAIT!! I know your curiosity switch is on again but let's go in sequence. So why do we want them?

I believe that unless one has loved an animal, part of one's soul remains unawake. For some, a Spirit Animal is an otherworldly guide who appears to offer love, healing, and support during difficult times, but for some, they are mere creatures wandering by the earth. Finding your spirit animal can radically change your life in countless, positive ways. Working with your animal spirit guide's 'energy' or 'medicine' can help enhance your mental, physical, emotional, and spiritual abilities. For me, spirit animals are as much as important as any other companion.

When you find your spirit animal you'll have a choice to make—either accept its messages, act on them, or walk away. If you accept your animal spirit guide's messages and act on them you might find your whole life-transforming. Finding your spirit animal and truly integrating its energy, medicine, and lessons into your existence is a spiritual awakening. Relationships, careers, thought patterns, tastes, anything which no longer serves your highest and best interest will fall away.

Having a spirit animal can help you increase your skills in life such as courage to leave a toxic relationship, ask for a raise, go to college, ability to communicate more effectively or speak your truth, path to tune into your psychic or intuitive self, strength to kick depression or addiction and find your joy and wisdom to make tough decisions.

Just like soul mates are cut from the same energy cloth as that of you, spirit animals also share the same energy as you. They are a part of your energy. Though we have animal spirit guides who do appear in our hour of need, it's our soul who cries out to the animal kingdom for help. Animal spirits hear those pleas and rally around us to offer protection, hope, healing, and wisdom.

Now, if you are reading this part carefully, that states the first reason why you need to know about your soul animal. When one is called to connect with their spirit animal it's a sign they're ready to evolve into their 'true or authentic self'. When you are called to find your spirit animal, you're searching for the part of your animal spirit which has been fragmented, injured, or lost.

I am sure I must have filled many overwhelming feelings in you and that is why it is the time when the most obvious question arises, which is how to find them? Well, I have done some research and have discovered a variety of ways to determine what exactly your totem (animal) is.

STEP 1: ATTEND AND OBSERVE

Be present in the current moment and observe what sync you have with nature. To become aware of your Spirit Animal, you must first become aware of the nature of animals. This helps you to forge a greater connection to nature, which you will need to identify your Spirit Animal. Pay attention to what animal or animals keep showing up in songs, pictures, movies, books, conversations, etc. Trust that if they keep appearing to you, they are trying to help you in some way. The key is to remain open, but not to force it. Once it is declared, it is important to stay aware of when a significant sign or messenger does cross our path. Note that it has to feel 'right': not every animal encounter or sign is significant. Make sure you feel into the experience when it happens rather than settling for whatever comes your way

STEP 2: THEY APPEAR IN DREAMS?

Humans often do not believe they are receiving messages from their spirit animal guides so they will come to us in the dream state. Often, it is much easier for folks to trust their dreams rather than their intuition during waking times or meditations. Spirit Animals are also said to contact us in our dreams. Look out for animals that seem to persistently appear while you sleep – this could be a sign of your Spirit Animal trying to manifest itself to you. Pay particular attention to the messages your dreams deliver and to the specific situations in which animals are present. Animals in dreams may symbolize deep-rooted feelings not fully acknowledged in waking hours, a feeling that you find "wild" or hard to control, and/or your most basic instincts and emotions.

STEP 3: MEDITATE

Again, meditation comes to the solution. It is said that our Spirit Animals often reveal themselves to the subconscious mind during practices such as meditation. It involves attaining an altered state of consciousness and the use of deep imagery or visualization with the specific intention of meeting your spirit animal guide(s). Record what animals you encounter in your meditations, dreams, and waking life. Look for patterns or recurrences of a specific animal or animals. Find a quiet and comfortable space. Close your eyes. Begin to relax and quiet your mind. Breathe deeply and slowly. If any thoughts come into your mind, let them drift away like clouds in a clear blue sky. Once your mind is completely still and empty, ask (silently with thought) and see what your spirit animal reveals. Be patient the way you were when you asked for your guardian angel to appear. And as soon as you see them or get any instinct, draw what you see and feel or write a description.

Any time an animal crosses your path, and you think "how peculiar," it is most likely a spirit animal! Take time to consider the meaning behind this interaction—it may carry a deeper meaning that could shed light on an area of your life that you're questioning. A poem defines it beautifully:

The way a crow
Shook down on me
The dust of snow
From a hemlock tree

Has given my heart
A change of moods
And saved some part
Of a day I had rued.

~Robert Frost

Everyone has a spirit animal, but not everyone is willing to try and find it. It takes time and patience to truly listen and let that animal come to you. Once you do, however, you will experience a deeper connection with nature and this planet through the harmony between yourself and your spirit animal. If you find out your spirit animal from some test on Google, you shall find what that animal stands for? Therefore, going forward you'll enter the world of mystic animals; fasten your seat belts reader 'cause you don't know what's coming next!

Now let me tell some features connected to animals we tend to see in our daily lives but reference the spirit animals I mention and pay special attention to any of the animals that you may have encountered recently. Their meanings may help determine their purpose for crossing your path:

1: BUTTERFLY

One of the most common animals we see. Spiritually speaking, the butterfly spirit animal signifies resurrection and the need for meditation if you wish to take the road to enlightenment. But perhaps the most well-known butterfly symbolism is that of rebirth, metamorphosis, and transformation. A butterfly stands for personal transformation, believed to be one of the most symbolic signs about transformation and profound change. Death and rebirth are present here—perhaps something in your old self dying away so a newer version of you can present itself. Butterflies also carry the message of "being light" and floating above earthly matters.

2: CAT

Standing for independence and curiosity, the cat shows up when action needs to be taken, and in essence, shows up for courage to. Those who have it as their spirit animal might want to start developing a strong balance between freedom and togetherness and get in balance with it. Patience and adventure are also attributes. The cat spirit animal is fanciful, magical, and independent, just like the lion spirit animal. The cat symbolism works in your life by appearing to you when you need self-confidence and reassurance

3: CROW

Very often, a crow is considered inauspicious but the animal stands for vision and intelligence. The crow brings a lot of magic and mysteries. Crows are known for their higher perspective, flexibility, and mostly their "trickster" personality types. If the crow has been coming to you—whether in an awakened state or dreams—consider your connection to life and its magic. If the crow has become your spirit animal, it helps you in transformation in your life and developing your vision. Crow represents destiny and higher perspectives.

4: HORSE

Freedom and passion for it are the main attributes of the horse. Among all the spirit animals, horse shows a strong motivation that carries one through life. The meaning of the horse showing up varies depending on whether this spirit guide is represented as wild, tamed, or moving freely, or constrained. The horse is known for being one of the most hardworking animals on earth, with the ability to carry on even on the roughest roads and the toughest climbs. The horse meaning signifies overcoming obstacles, and how you should carry yourself in the face of adversity.

5: BEAR

The animal stands for strength and confidence. Bears have been worshipped throughout time as a strong totem, filling people with the courage they needed to stand up and fight adversity. This spirit animal relates to the earth and nature and is able to guide people and support them through physical and emotional healing. It is also referred to as healing and provides strong grounding forces. This power animal will provide for support and strength. The bear is also a guide to take leadership in your life or in other people's lives. This animal is feared and admired for its strength. Its presence inspires respect. Its strength and powerful stature will inspire you to step into a leadership role in your life and act without fear.

6: EAGLE

Eagles are signals that it is the time to reconnect to your spiritual path. They are here to remind us to listen to our hearts and not rely on our minds so much. If an eagle is your animal, it means that you have lightness in you, but need to stay grounded. Eagles represent light, spirit, and healing—healing yourself so you can connect deeply to your spiritual journey. This spirit animal carries the knowledge of magic and gifts from above. They also represent how you should try and avoid drama. Eagle spirit animal is the messenger of the gods and the lord of the birds. There are sixty species of eagles around the world and copious legends in every culture to match. Eagle is synonymous with freedom, vision, and enlightenment.

7: WOLF

The wolf offers some of the most striking animal meanings in the realm of spirit animals. The power and strength of the wolf bring forth appetite for freedom, instinct, intelligence, and awareness of the importance of social connections. This animal can also symbolize a lack of trust and fear of being threatened. When the wolf shows up in your life, pay special attention to what your intuition is telling you. Perhaps your spirit animal is warning you about challenges with personal boundaries: You may feel you have exposed yourself too much with someone or in a certain situation and need to pull back or strengthen emotional or physical boundaries with that person or in the context of that experience.

8: OWL

The owl is one of the rarer spirit animals. If you happen to cross paths with an owl, it is a true sign from the universe. The owl as a spirit guide that represents wisdom, deep connection, and intuitive knowledge. When the spirit of this animal guides you, you can see the true reality, beyond illusion and deceit, you can see beyond the illusions created by our minds. When this guide comes to you, you might be at a time in your life where you are exploring the unknown—perhaps going through a transition or about to embark on a journey. When the owl is one of your power animals, you have a strong intuition and can access information and wisdom that's usually hidden to most. The spirit of this animal encourages you to look beyond deceiving appearances into the true reality of a situation or a person's motives.

9: SNAKE

A mysterious and often found unethical animal is snake. It is denoted for healing and transformation. When the snake spirit animal appears in your life, it likely means healing, opportunities, change, important transitions, and increased energy are manifesting. The snake animal's meaning is powerfully connected to primal energy and life force. In many cultures, it is referred to as a powerful totem representing the source of life.

10: LION

We often see the lion as the king of the wild and think of strength and courage which is quite right. The lion spirit animal represents strength in overcoming difficulties and courage. In the spiritual realm of spirit animals, the lion wins the prize for the most relentless fighter in the face of life challenges and holding them with courage. The presence of this power animal could also mean that something "wild" or difficult to control is happening or will happen. Personal power and assertiveness are also denoted by the lion.

11: HUMMINGBIRD

When a hummingbird is present for you, whether for your long periods of time or just for a day, try to connect with the enjoyment of life and try not to take things so seriously. They are here to remind us to be playful and that ultimately, the connection is what really matters—whether it is with loved ones or a higher power. Those who have the hummingbird as a totem are invited to enjoy the sweetness and candy-like feel of life, feel happiness, and lift up negativity wherever it creeps in and express love more fully in their daily endeavours. Hummingbird stands for the innocence in your life and positivity.

12: SPIDER

It is considered as an insect, often irritating and inauspicious. Well, actually spider promotes creativity and receptiveness. When you notice a lot of spiders coming up in your life or in your dreams, it is a reminder for you to create the life you want to lead. Spiders are known for creating intricate webs and patience for capturing their prey, so these guides are here to tell us when to start building the life we want. The spider is a remarkable figure of feminine energy and creativity in the spirit animal kingdom.

There are many more animals but certainly, if I start about them then I will have to write another book, but you can search about the animals anywhere there are very rare cases when they are misinterpreted. I have gathered all this information from all over the internet so that I can present a general view to you. The beauty of your spirit animal is the harmony that comes when two species connect. Your spirit animal can help you make tough decisions in your life or help you through a difficult period. Understanding the traits of your spirit animal can help you understand what traits you also have to help you throughout your life. When you search for how to harness their energy, people will come up with their own tried and tested ways but what I recommend is TRUST. Try to build a deeper connection with your spirit animal. Look for connections between its behaviours and your own. You will come across ways like don't humanize your spirit animal or try and use your new-found wisdom but, if you won't be able to open up to your spirit animal's appearance in life, you won't be able to figure any of this out.

Animals are auspicious, they have heart and soul. If they were to be useless, they won't be roaming all over the planet. A little off the topic request, please do not be cruel with animals, not for fun, not for any reason. They also feel. They cannot live and heal if we will come up like this. We don't do this to our angels or gods then why to them? They are equally important!

KINDRED SPIRITS

Nothing more than our relationships give value to our lives. We are socially living creatures who live and die by the connections we build with those around us. They give us meaning, purpose, and a reason to wake up when nothing else makes sense. They are our sources of showing compassion, happiness, and joy, and in many cases, our reason for living. But there are some people who will connect with so much more intimately and deeply than most. These are our kindred spirits.

Kindred spirits are individuals that resonate at the same level or frequency as us. As everything in life is composed of energy, we often feel attracted to some people and repelled by others. Kindred spirits often play a very passive role in our lives. In other words, they do not play a very major part of our spiritual growth, but they do comfort and support us. Often kindred spirits share the same personality types as us, as well as similar tastes, interests, and passions. While not all kindred spirit connections are necessarily deep and soulful, some can be (these can be thought of as "soul friend" connections).

Kindred spirits carry the magic of fireflies. They are like little lights that gravitate towards each other in life because they have harmonious energy. The likeness between you can be such that you feel like you've met another manifestation of yourself (although, this shouldn't be confused with sexual attraction, which also has a strong energetic pull). The connection is weird ... and wonderful!

Physically, a kindred spirit could be anything: a close friend, a confidant, a family member, a teacher, a lover, a pet, or even a landform. The relationship is a positive, supportive one. Kindred spirits will encourage each other to develop as people and offer positive energy to each other. They think in the same kind of way and share similar values and underlying understandings of the world. A kindred spirit connection will highlight our talents and our potential, fostering the very best parts of us and allowing us to grow as a person.

Some people would argue that you may very well have met them before, just in a previous life. Kindred spirits can also be soul connections and although we might actually be meeting a person for the first time, it could be it's just the first time in this incarnation. If you subscribe to the idea of previous lives, someone who you feel a particularly strong connection with maybe a person you've made a soul contract with. This is an agreement made before the current life where you agree with another soul to work together to test yourself and help your respective souls attain their goals.

Kindred spirits are special relationships… experienced variously from briefly felt moments of friendship to enduringly profound body-soul love and friendship connections. They need not necessarily be lovers. But technically, a kindred spirit can be someone you only met once, but they just "got" you at that moment and you just cannot resist the bond you made.

It has never been proven, but perhaps there might be a strong connection beyond words between people who understand and "get" each other and get along with the energy they carry. So if you think you might have a kindred spirit in someone new in your life, here are a few ways I believe you might be able to tell if someone is your kindred spirit. Keep in mind that this is just my opinion perhaps it might be different for different people. Keep in mind that these traits won't apply to every kindred soul connection. You have to trust your intuition, for the most part, but you can use this list of traits as a guide for common signs.

SIGN 1: SIMILAR PRINCIPLES

You're unlikely to have widely differing opinions on the soul or the afterlife. Similarly, you'll likely share similar views on controversial political topics such as the death penalty or abortion. Everyone's experience of life is subjective and related to their personal lessons and evolution, in addition to their personality and character traits. Kindred spirits tend to see life in the same way.

This is about the way you view life and humanity and this social race, and while you and your friends may have your general agreements and disagreements on certain issues, you have roller coaster conversations, your kindred spirit will generally understand the world the same way that you do. The bigger things in life will never be a point of conflict—you live your lives the same way, which is why you connect as intimately as you do. This makes it easy to share a person's company and to develop ideas about the world. Although you'll have differences, the alignment on major topics aligns with your general approach.

SIGN 2: RESPECT

Following on from the previous point, we have the concept of respect. On topics that you do disagree, you won't argue or fall out with this person if they are your kindred soul. Instead, you'll respect that you have different life experiences and so are likely to hold different opinions, but you will each respect the overall nature of one another.

You seem to always be in sync. There's a natural flow to your relationship. It just feels "easy" to be together. Both of you know that motivation, support, and encouragement are what the other person needs, which is why you will never be too quick to judge your kindred spirit in any sense. It's a supportive relationship, and you encourage each other to grow.

If a relationship lacks respect, it is almost certainly an unhealthy one. Toxic relationships nearly always have a lack of respect as a common element. Meaningful, healthy, and mutually beneficial relationships show mutual respect. It's fundamental.

SIGN 3: YOU NEED EACH OTHER

You add to each other's lives. You enjoy spending time together and feel relaxed. You're able to just be yourself. You feel happy, uplifted, and comforted just by being in each other's company. There might be moments where you will feel that no one in the world really cares about you or your problems. In those moments, your kindred spirit, your friend, will feel that they are needed and come rushing to your aid. Even if all you need is a hug. It could be that a simple phone call or an invite to go for a walk is exactly what the other person needs. This is no mere coincidence.

Kindred spirits are able to sense an imbalance in the other person's energy, even when neither person is aware of it. As such, you'll often find that you offer support to each other without knowing the specifics of the problem. Just as I always knew when my kindred spirit is avoiding everyone because she feels low and is not because she is busy. Kindred spirits have the uncanny ability to just know when one of their kindred spirits is in desperate need of help.

SIGN 4: FEELING OF BEING COMPLETE

There are parts of you that you've always known are weaknesses or you always tend to keep them covered. Perhaps you suffer a little too much from anxiety. Or you are always socially awkward. Whatever it is, it's like your kindred is good at those things. They love going out and they're cooler than the cucumber even in tense situations!

It's so easy to be together that neither of you feels the need to fill the empty space with words and you guys never have awkward silences. It doesn't matter what's happening and why it happened, you always support each other in and out. Everyone goes through tribulations that are hard to overcome, but you both make sure that you don't have to do it all alone. You provide solutions, support, and unconditional love which are impossible to break. Let's be honest, life is a bit of a game sometimes. But it's a game that you want your kindred spirit to win and cherish.

If you do not know about kindred spirits until now, but you think a person you know might be the one, trust me on this, before concluding or informing them, just sit back and cherish all the things they did for you and how much thankful you are to them. You will for sure have tears because there are so many emotions connected to that person and it becomes so overwhelming.

SIGN 5: BE YOURSELF

Again, authenticity is in action! You never feel to show the side of yours where you pretend. Kindred spirits don't feel the need to wear a mask around one another; it's one of the reasons that you'll feel so comfortable in their company. You'll be able to discuss aspects of your life that even your closest friends or family is completely unaware of.

It's almost like you understand exactly what the other one is thinking. It's hard to describe feelings in words. They're complex, flying balls of energy that can't be put into senses. But somehow, you "get" your partner's feelings, even if you can't articulate them. A simple look into each other's eyes says everything you need to know and deliver. And this is the same in different social situations and circumstances. It's like you know your partner's uncomfortable before they know they are themselves! It's a special connection that can't be put into words ever.

You learn from each other. You're open and honest. A kindred spirit could bring new perspectives and objectivity, and sometimes this will be challenging. But that's part of growing as an individual. You help each other move forwards on your personal life journeys.

However, they come into our lives, kindred spirit connections are to be cherished. They might seem like a rare thing but, if you're open, you may find the spark more often than you expect. When you are connected to someone who is your kindred spirit, you'll carry them with you or at least try your best to do so. You'll feel something you've never felt before and even though it might be scary and difficult to process, you need to pay attention to it. When you feel something in the pit of your stomach, you'll be worried that it's a sign that something is wrong, but that couldn't be further from the truth and in the end, it is all about growth.

Connection to your kindred spirit will find your longing and attachment for them wherever it is in you find yourself. Near or far, you'll feel the connection to them and wait madly for the time when you can be nearer to them once again. Kindred spirits have a special connection and link that others don't feel and can't always understand because you can't put that into words. You may find yourself feeling alone in a room full of people when your kindred spirit is not there, but you won't be alone in actuality.

While a kindred spirit can teach us to respect everyone's life paths, as well as better understand ourselves and our connections with others, they may not always have the strength of connection that characterizes a soul mate or twin flame. People generally get confused between whether it's a soul mate or a kindred spirit? This is a common question and for good reason. On the surface, it appears as if they're the same thing. But you'd be mistaken. Soul mate connections are unconditional, it's beautiful, its magical and soul mates are able to stick through tough times together. A kindred spirit can be a soul mate but will have a more dilute role.

The important distinction that's worth noting is the "twin flame" relationship. This is a very intense relationship that could be positive but could also be negative also. It's passionate and sexy in a good way. The relationship can be so strong that it can lead to intense feelings of love and heartbreak and compassion. If the rockiness of a twin flame relationship can be worked through, it really can be an incredibly intense and meaningful and beautiful relationship. But generally, people make that difference between their kindred spirit and twin flames.

If you want to find your kindred spirit, I believe that you need to be who you truly are, who you truly admire. Let yourself live your best life by letting go of stuffy and stressful social norms and figuring out what works for you and your inner being. When we think about what makes us happy, we frequently reference external and material things: money, success, a nice home, car, family, etc but there is a lot of happiness that can come from within. I believe that happiness is stifled, however, when we are not true to ourselves and don't let our inner selves come out to play, we miss out on that happiness.

PART III

INVIGORATE YOU

The spiritual journey is the unlearning of fear

And acceptance of love

It is reality that awakens possibilities

But it needs guidance just like a dove

There will come a time when you feel all this is dark

At that point you need to be nourished

'cause that is when you make your actual mark

Upon awakening, let the words Thank you flow from your lips

This is just a little piece of advice, some tricks, and tips.

~Priyal Bansal

SPIRITUAL AWAKENINGS

In this world, many of us think practically and many of us prefer to go with the flow. But have you ever experienced something supernatural? Now, this doesn't mean any ghost encounters but anything that feels so pure or which feels out of your control, working from within. I am sure there must be some experiences like this. If not, then wait for the right time.

So, what is spiritual awakening? Is it having some powers suddenly, like a witch? Is it like doing black magic? Remember the new bright world I talked about at the end of the first unit? Yes, this spiritual awakening is the door to this world. My definition for spiritual enlightenment is the complete dissolution of one's identity as a separate self with no trace of the egoist mind remaining. Spiritual awakening is what I call the actual wakeup alarm.

A spiritual awakening represents the lifting of the veil of ignorance or avidya, which in Sanskrit means "incorrect understanding." Fortunately, though, the process of spiritual awakening runs directly counter to the currents of avidya in your life. The evolution of consciousness generates a forward pull, a momentum toward growth, transformation, and change that is one of the most powerful forces in the universe. Like a spaceship achieving escape velocity, spiritual awakening punches you out of the limiting gravity well of ignorance and push towards the ultimate destination of cosmic self-realization.

It's the beginning of something so beautiful and pure that none of us experience in our life before this. An instinct toward spirituality and a pull towards this appears to be deeply ingrained in humans. We can't help but keep on asking big questions: Research finds that even declared religious skeptics can't restrain a sense that there is something greater than the physical world they see. An explosion of understanding about reality and spiritual truths is where I mark the beginning of this process. Spiritual awakenings happen as a natural product of your Soul evolving, expanding, and maturing. Just as everything in life grows, so too does our connection with our Souls. As the brain processes sensory experiences, it naturally looks for patterns and signals- and our conscious selves often seek meaning in those patterns.

Getting spiritually attached to this world for the first time feels like you have met your soul. You feel face to face with your divinity. But the flip side to this is that when you attract the intensity of this divinity then you are forced to all that is untrue about yourself. This can be childhood experiences, lies that you keep telling yourself or pretending a masked self to others. And you have to start accepting all that about yourself, all that you ignore about yourself.

Your soul is connected to this world means establishing a link between you and your invisible saviours. So, you might be wondering whether you are already awoken or not? If yes, then why I did not realize it?

To answer these questions, I have deciphered a 5-stage awakening path which most of us go through. Now before I tell those stages here's a little disclaimer, the path may not unfold in the way I organized it but it's for sure that we all go through these stages when the time is right. Also few of the stages might overlap each other, that is they might occur at the same time, and also it is possible that you go through one stage multiple times, so do not panic, it's completely fine and your path is not dysfunctional.

Yes, so the stages I have noticed are:

1: Morning Alarm

2: Fairy Tale World

3: Dark Night

4: Oblivion

5: Grounded

But before explaining these stages there are few symptoms to talk about. Now, this does not mean that if you feel any of these symptoms then you are going through an awakening, there can be other reasons so do consult a doctor. So some spiritual awakening symptoms are that you feel as though your life is false, You start craving for meaning and purpose, You begin asking deep questions, You see how unhappy most people are, You thirst for authenticity and truth, You become aware of your old negative habits, You experience anxiety and/or depression, You become more sensitive, You want to make the world a better place, You deeply want to understand who you are, Your intuition is heightened, More synchronicity and a world full of loving humans.

Physical symptoms as water retention, bloating, weight gain, body pains, and mental disturbances like depression or hallucinations, your senses get magnified, weird sleeping patterns; you crave a certain food, and a healthy lifestyle. And your personality may also change.

So, these are certain symptoms and signs people generally go through. Now let's tap into what stages I have been talking about. And before you read about them all I will say is that the most important thing on this journey is PATIENCE.

MORNING ALARM

"When we quit thinking about ourselves and our self-preservation, we undergo a truly heroic transformation of consciousness."

The first stage of this spiritual awakening is a wake-up call from the spirits attached to your soul. At the beginning of this stage we do not have a specific process or intuitions or to-do list. A call to adventure is the spark that triggers a spiritual awakening. Every life has a moment, if seized that will change that life forever. The call to adventure is an awakening incident, a new perception that compels you to look at life differently. This wake-up call comes generally through two ways that I know. First is going through some tragedy. This is when you go through some traumatizing experiences be it personal, professional, in a family, or losing someone and that is when you try to find a way to get out of it and make yourself introduced to spiritual knowledge or spirituality. The second is something people generally ignore. So, do you feel someday to just open Google and search about your horoscope? If yes then there may be chances you snoozed your alarm. Basically, in this type you suddenly one day wish to dig down to the roots of your soul and this spiritual world. Maybe while/after reading my book you start your spiritual awakening.

Once you have answered the call to adventure, you step into a larger world. You become a conscious participant in your spiritual growth and evolution. Responsibility becomes the operative word as you begin to navigate your life toward opportunities that further expand your awareness. A subtle shift in perception has taken place and everything feels the same and oddly different simultaneously.

There are all kinds of heart openings, mind openings, body openings, energy openings, and psychic openings that people have. What they all can be are inspirations to go deeper on the spiritual path and to go within. You start to perceive reality in a completely different way. In this stage, you start seeing through the lies and delusions propagated by society. This is the first step in the journey of a spiritual seeker. One must not follow the path followed by his forefathers and should cleanse his heart before embarking on this spiritual journey. Patience and ardour are the major keys to traverse this valley.

To invoke this experience, I suggest the path I went through, there are many other ways you can go through like having a breakdown, fatigues, no signs, or spiritual feelings, etc, etc. But I like to choose mine because I believe that the path we choose changes our life accordingly. Therefore, my path was shown to me by my teacher, she told me to be positive first. And let me tell you I was so fascinated by all these spirit talks that I was ready to practice at least this. So, I prepared my mind to be positive for the forthcoming weeks and to sync with my heart.

When you become this much positive that you tend to see the positive side of every situation automatically then it's the best time for you to start the actual number 1 stage, start asking for signs!

Also, notice something during this positive-vibe-generation-time that you might feel someone assists you through the journey. This is not mandatory that you feel but if you feel then it's great. I felt this and I knew how amazing this feels. So, these invisible people or spirits or assistants are what we call our guardian angels. They are our messenger to god or this universe.

Ask them to give you signs; signs like to show you some number or to show you some animal, feather, dish, or whatever. Just ask them as “angels show me so and so thing if you are here with me”. Isn’t that fascinating?

And believe me on this when you see that sign you asked for it’s the best feeling in the world. You feel alive. I went for a sign as a feather.

With this the morning alarm just goes off, I mean this stage ends here generally. There isn’t any specific timeline for this period but on average it’s a couple of weeks. Besides, once a transformative and deeply awakening incident has been experienced, there can be no going back. Your eyes have been opened and you can’t un-see the vision of the higher reality calling to you, no matter how much you might want to deny it.

FAIRY TALE

What comes in your mind when I say fairy tale? Cinderella, rainbows, cupcakes, prince charming and a happily ever after, right?

And that is what exactly you will feel when you enter this stage. I call this bliss stage too. For those who went through the trauma period, it simply feels so good to get a clean drink of water, without any garbage and trauma after drinking the raw sewage of fear, lust, anger, jealousy and so forth your whole life. The more you drink this water, the more it simply becomes your natural state.

When you enter here you feel alive for the first time, you feel guided for the first time ever, and you feel as if everyone suddenly loves you and want to be with you. When I went through this stage it felt as if I was the saviour with a sword in my hand and my only purpose was to help others and save them—like a fighter, yes.

Do you know why you feel so? You feel this cloud nine experience because for the first time your soul is in action. You may say that it's impossible, we run every day because of the soul inside us, right? Well, that's what I also thought; unless you experience this you won't know how it feels. For the first time, it feels as if every cell in your body is dancing on your favourite song.

Everything feels so magical and you start feeling compassion, love, kindness, cheerfulness, and happiness because your energy system starts to expand. You feel everything because your heart is in the lead. You start connecting more to your intuitions and feelings. And you realize certain signs from the universe that you haven't received ever, and you notice some special gifts you have about which you never knew.

Note: To let this bliss happen you have to surrender yourself! You need to affirm your angels to step in your lives and use their magic wand to fix it. Angels cannot help you until it's your choice. I affirm them by saying" angels I truly trust you and I allow to enter in my life as and when you see fit".

You may turn up and ask me that am I doing something wrong or unlawful by letting them do so? Let me explain to you, this may sound philosophical but there is nothing like doing wrong, If you think something like that, it's your ego talking. If you do something even after it feels so wrong then trust me mate you are meant to do that. The more tuned into this space you are, the more you can see what is or is not appropriate for you.

This fairy tale stage is basically to rejuvenate your soul, after a long sleep. This is just a toast to positive things. Now, this is not necessary that you go through this bliss as the second stage. It could be any one of the 5. This stage too does not have a specific period, but it lasts maximum a month or so. But the thing to note here is that when you get access to all these things and positivity and energy you also get access to some special gifts, although everyone doesn't need to have those gifts but still what is most important is that we do not feel highly privileged or superior or unique. When these types of feelings come then this may ruin things, so just keep a watch in your attitude and try to be humble and generous to everyone.

At this point, you may set out to find a new way—a new philosophy, a different tradition, or practice that will help to contextualize or re-map your worldview. This is when many begin spiritual exploration in earnest. Often marked by a period of information gathering, self-study, and delving into world religions or psychology, you are drawn to practices and methods that align with your unique personalities and dispositions.

As I said, everyone's awakening is different. As you come to those resting points, you may suddenly feel incredibly normal. That's great. That's part of the integration. If you are truly allowing the awakening, you are integrating the bliss state into your everyday consciousness. Now, what's interesting about is that when you integrate into a state of awareness, you won't notice it as being anything special. This fairy tale starts but also has to end.

DARK NIGHT

So as the bliss stage ends, the dark night of the soul starts. This is a period where we go underground. This is like a time when everything starts to disorientate, especially in the starting when everything used to be so perfect and suddenly you don't know where your angels just vanished. You will feel as if everything just stopped. The spiritual path is not without struggle, however.

As such, going through the Dark Night is not a pretty or manicured experience—at its core, it's raw, primal, and the most difficult experience known to humanity. The Dark Night of the Soul is a period in life when we feel completely cut off from God or the Divine. The more aware you become of your disconnection from the Divine, the more chances you have of experiencing a Dark Night.

So, the dark night is the time when you need to heal. Healing is the removal of barriers we have to access god. It is the period to heal your entire karmic imbalance and all the toxic feelings you carried with you from your past lives. This is a time when we let go of old attachments to pain and false ego beliefs. If we let go of just a little of this junk, we can feel like we've struck gold.

Growth can be an uncomfortable process at times. As your chosen path challenges, you to change thoughts, emotions, speech, or behaviour to be more expansive, compassionate, forgiving, or kind, it is not uncommon to struggle with being in this world but not of it. Worse yet are the external influences that assault the spiritual seeker with temptations to give up the quest for awakening and return to a conventional life.

The soul intentionally triggers this dark night to put you out of the cycle of karma and all the junk you have from the past life. This happens because all the pain and suffering and karma are holding your soul back, so the soul consciously triggers dark night so that you can come out of this vicious cycle.

What to do now? How to access all that bliss again? I'll suggest waiting!

Wait and feel this moment, doesn't it feel as if you are normal again? As if you are back to feel like a human? Enjoy this moment of free flight. Enjoy this spaciousness. Watch the mind if it is trying to define and jump out and control life once more. Because if it is so, then darling you should remember how positive and strong you will be once you pass this. If you have stepped out of an old issue, don't be too quick to fill up that vacated space. Take your time.

But you still don't know what to do right? The ego is still in control and pops up every minute even after letting go of an issue, and that ego wants direction and definition. However, sometimes we don't need to do anything. Life is already on its path taking us where we need to go. This feeling also arises because in stage 2 you felt like guided for the first time and everything seemed to be in place and all that disappeared suddenly without any prior statement just like a breakup without any closure.

Witnessing and getting them into sense with those new realizations is an important part of going deeper into the work and becoming more stable in this process. If a person stops accepting and tries to resist the truth they're discovering, then spiritual development grinds to a halt until the issue that is resisting is addressed and solved.

At this stage, you may feel lost or helpless, as if you have succumbed to spiritual blindness and see yourself in a black room. However, what you often don't realize is that this blindness or challenges are the deceptions of your ego—your small self that fears its extinction in the ever-expanding field of spirit. Seen in this way, your spiritual challenges, or dark nights of the soul, become your spiritual teacher. Ram Dass would say, "Grist for the mill of enlightenment." Every setback then becomes an expression of your inner doubts and fears—trials and hurdles on your personalized and self-made obstacle course.

The dark night also gives us time to take a moment and figure out who we are. The more aware someone is, the more clearly they see about themselves and others.

So uncertainty in your spiritual practice may arise, but generally speaking to yourself, meditation, breathing to relax the body, being the witness to your experiences, and a little bit of energetic support (can be by you to you) goes a long way with the majority of issues. Another way that I often suggest is to sit and tap at your sternum (bone at the middle of the chest) with the rhythm of the heart. This one is scientifically proven because your soul resides in your heart, so as much as you connect to your heart the more you connect to your soul. Other practices may become close to useless, but the ones I mentioned tend to stick around for a longer period of time. Generally, after that, people make their own routines.

This experience, like any experience, is transitory. As I said before it is not compulsory that every one of us goes through this stage but generally we got some of the other forms of the dark night. It lasts for a couple of months or maybe years, but it will pass. That's okay. The more you go within this, the more you learn to be at peace with whatever experience life tosses your way and the fear of unknown experiences can dissolve through the path.

OBLIVION

Tell me what do you need after a long tiring journey? After hiking all week? Of course, rest! I call this stage oblivion because it brings in a sense of void and unconsciousness. It brings in fatigue because of all that karmic waste you have just dumped. Now try imagining a baby's delivery, the mother needs rest after giving birth and so does the baby. This is because the mother went through extreme pain and the baby just got a life!

This is somehow the same in this case, you need rest, and you need to find your roots in this phase. After a long dark journey, this comes in as a deep nice sleep. This is your body shutting down because you are completely overloaded with pain. You are being forced to deal with your pain through collapse rather than the arising of awakened awareness.

A permanent shift has taken place and you awaken fully to your true identity—the infinite, immortal, unbounded, God-force existing everywhere and in everything. You wake up fully to being the divine observer—the ever-present witness-self of the entire universe. It is in general, a total transformation of the heart, body, mind, and subtle energy. It can be a good time to find a spiritual caretaker to look after your basic needs through this profound shift.

But I generally do not consider this as awakening because there are plenty of reasons to feel tired or restless, so just before you conclude be sure that there isn't any physical issue as having an improper diet, or sleeping 4-5 hours only after doing zillion of things. To come at a decision, the intuitions, or feelings you may feel are being tired after sleeping the whole day, you'll feel loved, but you don't want to talk to anyone, and one important thing is feeling stillness which means you can sense time passing by.

At this stage you breakthrough to a new stage; visionary, transcendent, and sight beyond sight. This stage wants to see the power of letting things go and wants to overcome the resistance your ego has to stop this spiritual awakening but inside your soul--the real you have already chosen this path and vowed to move on with this. And you need to come into acceptance of it in reality. If you don't, then you're still resisting the change and disobeying it. It's time to let go of that resistance. It's exhausting and holding you back. Resisting your spiritual awakening will take away every last bit of energy you have until you can't get off the floor and people are deciding to put you in a mental asylum.

The biggest things that many people found to help through the fatigue have been meditation and other energetically supportive tools like yoga. But even these only go so far. So much of shifting is allowing, and then engaging in making changes that feel true to your heart after allowing. Although I was never able to meditate completely, call it a lack of interest or whatever. I preferred the other two ways which were: one—you do what makes you feel relaxed as for me listening to music and singing along is the best therapy and two—the sternum meditation I mentioned earlier.

Now I prefer these because they connect us to our souls. Our souls reside in our heart and connect to your new-born soul and nourishing it, knowing it, and relaxing with it is all what I feel is needed. Also, in many cases, while meditating or tapping your sternum bring you in contact with all your soul community, angels, and Spiritual power.

One of the biggest things people have trouble with is explaining to others what their needs are during these shifts. I encourage a lot of people to have journals so that they can understand what's going on and make a sense of it. Until you can explain to yourself what's going on in your own words, you won't be able to explain it to anyone else. I feel this is the most needed thing because during this shift many people would leave you because things are not working out, but somewhere deep down I believe this is the whole purpose of this stage, to show you on what rotting foundation you are trying to build your relationship. And trust me on this, when at the last you see those 2-3 faces who have stuck around you throughout, then it'll be the best feeling as if you are being rewarded by god to pass this exam.

And also, because awakening can move a lot of energy, people often have their sleep disrupted, insomnia and that disruption can lead to a lot of fatigue and tiredness. There's a whole list of ways that people no longer sleep normally as the initial shifts and transformation roll through. Night-time and psychic visions and sudden abilities to have out-of-body experiences are some of the things that can change someone's sleep as their hidden talents start to emerge, thanks to the awakening. I would surely like to give some light on this, well I too have psychic abilities and know how it feels to have both good and bad dreams come true. Do you ever feel déjà vu, but cannot tell if you ever had such experience in person? If yes, then my friend you may also have some of these abilities all you need is to tap them so that they get activated.

The last piece of advice for this stage is that spiritual awakening is never about punishing you. Nothing is going wrong. You are transforming. Although this phase lasts for years eventually things are going very right, perhaps for the first time in your life. All the suffering that you perhaps didn't know was there coming up to be processed and released so that you can be happy, healthy, and whole and manifest the greatest of things. As you heal, you can open further and go deep down. Deeper wounds can be illuminated, and your spiritual growth can expand you even more like a free bird.

GROUNDED

"As I entered this world, I would leave behind the nurturing of my family and my home, but in other sense, I would take their protection with me. The lessons I have learned, the feelings of being grounded and belonging that have been woven into my character there would be my companions on the journey."

~Sidney Poitier

By this time, you have evolved a lot, you have experienced how life tastes. Grounded is a stage for me where we completely enter into our new life with an expanded energy system and mature self. Here we feel like a grown-up person whereas in stage two it felt like a teenager tasting freedom for the first time.

Try and imagine this stage like a tree, you stabilize your roots in this stage so that you can handle your immense size. You become more stable in not only your energy system but also emotionally and mentally and spiritually. This is a very beautiful time.

Also, here you experience all the connection again with your guides and god. By the time we come to this stage we feel the bliss again but the way we want to enjoy that bliss and have an exciting and happy life again we also want to go out to the world like a normal human again. Here we accept all the changes and the path we are on and mix it with our everyday life.

We are grounded in life, we know it's okay if we are feeling good or bad, it is okay if we are happy or sad, it is okay if we are angry, or we are feeling the love. we live life with beauty and fulfilment. An increasing sense of light-heartedness, with consistent spiritual practice, happiness, and joy becomes your ground state. You take life less seriously. Hysteria and melodrama have less influence over you. Care freeness and detachment flow from you spontaneously and you feel much more at ease in life.

In this stage, we implement all the spiritual lessons we have learned in our spiritual awakening. We are ready by this stage to ground our lessons more and start our civilization all over again. We focus on shedding away negative emotions, biases, and judgments so that we could see life more clearly and we become less emotional in decision-making.

Our energy system expands and becomes more magnetic. We are super active and super magnetic at the end. We no longer feel fragile or depressed. This is because when we ground energy we send it back to the earth, to be grounded can also mean to have a good understanding of energy use. The energy of mind, body, and soul the source energy must be in balance and harmony for life. As our roots go down and down we get back the guidance and the connection we had with our angels and that becomes stronger. You become a very powerful manifester. And all those feelings I was talking about in stage two about love and compassion return back to you whereas you were feeling nothing of them in the previous two stages- isn't that cool?

But you know what the difference is? There in stage two you were in a fairy tale and now in stage five you are more in reality, you feel the oneness. You start understanding that people have a reason why they behave so, they have some experiences and stories. You began to see that life is a purely subjective experience and therefore your judgments of others said nothing about them and said everything about yourself.

The timeframe for this one is generally years and years because you need to ground which means your thoughts, your actions, your habits, your beliefs, your hobbies, your work, your everything is aligned with each other. It means that you know what do you stand for and what you do not stand for. It means you know what your values are, and you are moving from those values. It means that you know what you value in other people, and you only allow people with the same values to come into your life. It means that you speak from a place of compassion toward others, but you still stay grounded into your own beliefs without compromising them with anyone or anything.

So as this is the last stage of awakening, the first question arises is what next? When you are done grounding your energy and lessons and start implementing them in regular lives then you encounter the path for your life mission. The whole purpose of you being here, in this world, starts to come to you after this path. You become healthier and your heart is more confident, and you start moving towards what you are here to achieve. Although you do not know what your full purpose or meaning is until the last breath you can surely look back to your experiences and path to collect the bits about your mission. The path of spiritual awakening is the grandest adventure you can ever undertake. You are deeply privileged just to recognize the truth that such a journey stand before you. And embracing it is nothing less than following the heroic call of your life purpose and destiny. You walk with great purpose. You don't need to know what that purpose is, but you take one step ahead every day to that mission. And with this, you follow your life and start realizing what you actually are.

AFTERLIFE

Life after spiritual awakening: Enlightenment or Spiritual awakening is regarded as the end of Knowledge? A state of total spiritual awareness. But is it? Is Spiritual Awakening a destination or an endless pursuit? To sustain a perpetual state of spiritual awakening, there's a lot that still needs to be done.

If you're in the throes of a spiritual awakening, it can sometimes feel like the world has turned upside down. All of a sudden, you have a new perspective on life, and see everything with a fresh set of eyes. While this can be an amazing, wonderful experience, it can also be quite scary. It can seem as if everything you've known, and everything you've worked for, is suddenly in jeopardy.

Awareness finds itself spreading forever in a warm and very accepting space. Meanwhile, we are living in a world full of boundaries and people who judge. From personal boundaries to national borders, our everyday world is all about fences. From the reality of spreading seemingly forever in great peace, people who have had a spiritual awakening find themselves back into a world full of boundaries, fences, rules, and expectations, a place where everyone carries their personal constitution. The spiritual realm is about unconditional, overwhelming, and passionate love. Almost by definition, an awakening is to find love and more love, and intimacy beyond words and a wave of peace beyond experience.

Meanwhile, we live in a world where love can be a one-night stand or can be a material attachment. Love is very rarely found without some condition today. We live in a world where judging others is much more common and important than finding the humility to look inward at ourselves and find kindness and compassion for all and we neglect the need to grow individually. Spiritual awakening is discovering a world in which its very essence is to spread kindness and compassion.

There are vastness and great freedom of thought, feeling, and movement in a spiritual awakening, the sense of reconnection, and recognition. Life is true and has essence without limits. But once back in our normal world, life feels very confining because we are left with few choices. Creativity suddenly has narrowed, and the physical world can be like shackles on the power of love, imagination and you can be sad seeing the scenario. There is such a big difference between the expansive spiritual encounter and being confined again to all the rules and limits of normal hustle and bustle. A practical life of thinking and doing can be so contrary to a world of fiery beauty and simply being all about love and where peace exists in all situations. Awareness is set free in spiritual awakening and is challenged, and you feel compromised coming back where it is much about just getting through the chores of the day.

The experience for many people in spiritual awakening includes meeting their soul family, spirit guides, and yes, of course, angels. We have come home and found comfort. The family is reunited and is found waiting, and excited. It is our spiritual family. We have finally come home at peace, and we do not want to leave. While on our Earthy journey, people are looking for their soul mate or soul family, but to see it broad-mindedly, on the other side everyone is a spiritual partner.

The question here arises is what about life after? What steps to follow? To be honest, while I am writing this book I do not know what happens after the process. Everyone's life has different paths and has a different process than what I had.

The first and perhaps most important point to grasp as you're beginning your life after the spiritual awakening process is that nothing needs to happen. Often, when we first begin to open our eyes, we feel the strong calling of a new way of life. While this is joyful, for some it can also come with a sense of duty or obligation. You may feel compelled to take actions you're not comfortable with because you begin to prioritize your spiritual progress over your material world.

It is very possible to have a deep internal transformation, and yet still maintain the same job and career you've always had. This is especially true if you have always enjoyed your work and find it meaningful and fulfilling. However, far more likely is that some of us have just awakened and just started burning up in the consciousness and awareness that you think you are ready to rebuild. You are not. If your awakening was yesterday or even four months ago, you probably don't even know yourself as there is an identity crisis. You probably had a moment of awakened understanding and from that moment a certain kind of experience with different feelings, emotions, and realizations came. But that is just the tip of the proverbial iceberg.

For those of you in the aftermath of three to six years of intense inner change, you probably already have some things growing in your life and you must be experiencing deep peace. Other parts of your life may need active rebuilding. But what does rebuilding even mean in a world so temporary and fake? First of all, try to let that intense fire die down that you had during the process. You won't have been able to work with certain issues, and you'll have to heat the kiln for those at a later point. This isn't bad, it's normal. It's just something that happens. We are a species that is deeply attached to a lot of things, including ideas and old pain.

The best way to live life after a spiritual awakening is to embrace and admire the experience. This may throw the old life into vain as one seeks new work, activities, friends, maybe even a new partner, and obviously a new personality. But once the heart has been opened there is only one choice, and this is to receive the love, blessings, and signals and continue loving.

In spiritual awakening colours are more vivid and bright, thoughts are clearer, the wall of the mind has been broken down opening true awareness. During this experience, doubts, worries, and unnecessary desires, hopes, and problems, all the junk normally floating in and blocking the mind are gone. Awareness without all the material stuff and normally occupying it is brilliant like sunshine light. Now there are new opportunities to meditate and continue the clearing by receiving our peaceful heart and keeping mind in sync. The spiritual awakening experience is an introduction to our awareness in its natural, true state but does not forget to keep you in touch with the material world.

At the end of the day, however, spiritual growth is about learning to move in greater alignment with your intuition. Once you become clear about how to follow your intuition and receive inner guidance, you can begin to make decisions in accordance with that guidance. Trusting this new form of knowledge takes practice. Over time, you may find it leading you into new work opportunities and jobs you had never previously considered. You will know if and when it's time for a change based on this intuition. When you feel a positive sense of expansion and fulfilment, you will know you are on the right path. You will begin to visualize your success, and the right choice will appear obvious to you, and the universe will begin to conspire in your favour.

Another thing that you can do is, observe yourself. Learn about yourself. Human beings are fascinating. When we get out of our way, we often flow towards the things that are most meaningful or supportive without labelling such beliefs to those things. When you embrace your leaning and sit back to observe and admire yourself, you get to know how and what you want your further life to be. This is very different than the concept of thinking out what you want in materialistic things. I can't say that you won't be able to do that too. The awakened space embraces and triggers all forms of human curiosity. No tool or human ability is left out. They're all available to you every time. What I am describing is one way to notice what you want to create in your life and how you want to create it. It works when you aren't stuck in old unconscious and ego patterns, which is why this is a difficult tool to use when you are early in your inner work after a spiritual awakening.

Life is not about the big things which our minds ponder on always but the little ways we lift one another and humanity. The good life after a spiritual awakening is to remember to turn inward again and again for the answers and more importantly to question the pure substance which makes life worth living and worth loving. Here we are reminded that we are a spiritual soul. The inner world which many have had a glimpse of in a spiritual awakening is a message for all of us to keep looking for a good and being able to keep that hope, to absorb the heart essence in ourselves and in life itself and actually draw all your attachment towards this life. There is so much understanding and peace to realize after the awakening. There is a new frontier. Life after a spiritual awakening is not how much we do in the world but how much love we can do within us for ourselves. We are called to be an anchor of love and humanity. The presence of love and purposefulness are the same.

As I write the ending of the book, I want you to join hands with me to a better, loving, and peaceful society. Let us create a sense of belongingness among each other. What you do after you grow spiritually is a personal experience, but the basic purpose of spirituality remains the same for all. I am grateful for how spiritual learning made me realize that this world is so sensitive. Let's use our knowledge and create peace. With this, I raise a toast to a better, loving, caring, kind, and a family-like world.

TOP 7 QUESTIONS

After having this knowledgeable journey, you will surely have some more questions which are left unanswered. Well, I promised you in the beginning only that, I won't let you step out of this book without complete insight.

And with this questionnaire, I also intend to ignite that fire of curiosity so that you go out and find what all is still left to be discovered. Questions are far more important than answers. Answers come to us constantly. But answers are responses to questions we're constantly putting out. If you can consciously ask the right questions, the answers you seek will naturally appear. Little fragments of curiosity that gets at the narrow of important issues that resonate and thrum and linger. Statements of opinion, answers, and other lies are fine, provided they move aside to let the questions through.

Plus, answers aren't destinations. They actually lead to more questions. And it's in posing the right questions where the true A-HA moments come. Wisdom is not about having the right answers, but in asking the right questions. The wisest people have more questions than answers.

Now stop reading. Meditate on these. Ponder them and allow the knowing within to blossom.

Q1. Can you start your awakening by yourself?

In my experience, in fact, in anyone's experience, this question is certain to arise. The truth is that you cannot start any spiritual process only on your mind's wish. No spiritual process will ever come to fruition if your only purpose is to satisfy your mind. And, let me tell you that processes like a spiritual awakening or an awakening do not happen if you are not ready to take that. As I clearly mentioned that it is not all about flowers blossoming, so your soul or destiny will not put something in front of you if you can't overcome it. Thereby, you cannot start awakenings before you are actually ready.

Q2. Is there any end to spiritual awakening?

Awakening is a process or cycle. This will eventually end and a new one will start. Although no one is sure if there is ever an end to spiritual awakening because this process is all about being grounded and healing you. Often spiritual awakening happens so spontaneously that many people are confused by what is happening to them. But yes, as I mentioned in every phase, what time frame they need, it is probably certain that it takes a couple of years to complete the basic process. It's not easy to go through it but once we're done we become completely new stronger versions of ourselves. No matter how dark and lonely your journey may seem at times, remember that you are never alone.

Q3. What are prominent changes after awakening?

As you evolve spiritually, you become more alive. Your soul starts to fly like a bird. Your heart feels so open and you actually feel the love flowing through your blood. You will have more compassion, not only for the ones you know but also for the people you don't. Self-love heightens. You cannot love the world if you don't love yourself.

You feel so much grounded than ever before, and you can never be a narcissist even if you choose to be. You know that you are heavenly loved and blessed.

A very soothing change after awakening is that you stop running from life. Especially if you went through the dark night multiple times, you must have isolated yourself to cut off all the emotions that flow through your energy field. Well, after awakening you become more grounded and stable. Your energy field is still sensitive, but you know how to handle this now.

And you feel a deep peace. A peace that no one can ever break. You have sowed this seed so deep that you will always have a sense of soothing even in the state of anxiety.

Q4. How can we have peace and anxiety both at the same time?

I know this question will pop up after reading the previous answer, but the thing is that the peace you will feel after the cycle is complete will be worth than any other thing in this material world. This peace is a feeling and emotion of heart whereas, on the other hand, anxiety is superficial. It is an illusion of the mind. When you are in anxiety and think about this anxiety, you will know that this will pass away, and it is temporary.

Q5. Do we lose our identity? Why?

This is not certain whether you will lose your identity or not but yes, people go through a loss. The reason being that you enter a high level of vibration, and you cannot reach that level until you let go of rigidity. All that rigidness that you have needs to go. So the mental constructs of our mind about our identity do not like to change and therefore is not acceptable.

And another reason for this identity loss can be your ability to see the deeper truths. As you start with your spiritual awakening, you see the veiled side of everything and as you move on with your spiritual journey, you actually do not feel any need to hold on to any identity.

Q6. What does an identity collapse look like?

When you lose your identity, you really don't know if that's true or it is some delusion. The common changes or symptoms a person goes through are that they feel completely lost, they cannot find any purpose and are not able to sense change or anything.

You tend to become very anxious and restless. Obviously, when your mental construct falls down, it is perfectly normal to feel anxious. Also, your worldview changes. Your likes and dislikes, places you want to go, or the things you wanted to accomplish in life can change.

You no longer like to justify yourself. There is a sense of frustration, and you feel stuck every time you try to explain yourself, so you just don't feel like defining your attributes. Another most common sign is that you start over thinking a lot. When your mind can no more sense than construct is made, it goes on a search for a substitute model

Q7. How to overcome identity loss?

This identity loss can be very disturbing and can probably be your worst nightmare. You need to work out it with yourself, so you need to let go of this frustration and anxiety. You need not try to revive yourself; all this is happening for your higher purpose.

You need to become comfortable with the change. Get familiar with the fact that life is not about permanent and constant things. And a piece of very major advice is not to accept projections. People around you will notice this change and will project their emotions on you, but you need not take that energy and be clear, you can go and say them that," I am going through a spiritual process for good, please give me some time." Or whatever you want, but please are clear.

ACKNOWLEDGEMENTS

Presenting gratitude to someone is the biggest form of respect you can give someone. The very first thought I had when I wanted to write this book was to present this as a vote of thanks to my angels and universe. They have been my constant support throughout my life. They are the ones who triggered my spirituality. I wanted to thank my knowledge and wisdom. My angels on earth were, Mansi ma'am, my soul teacher who helped me unravel every aspect of this book. From motivating me to making biggest decisions for this book, she did everything possible. Thank you ma'am for being my inspiration. Furthermore, I would thank my parents for believing in my and actually supporting me in and out. Their expectations from me pushed me hard. All the resources they presented me and all that they did is truly appreciable. My friends also played an active role. Garvita who is my twin flame boosted up my enthusiasm and helped me to write this book. I present my gratitude to her. Sanjana, who is my best friend, acted like a strong critic and made me realize my mistakes and error.

Thank you Inkfeathers for believing in me and guiding me through the process. I may not be able to find any more supportive publishers anywhere else.

I am eternally grateful to all those who worked with me and made my dream an actualization. Your support and efforts were a perfect motivation.

ABOUT THE AUTHOR

Being a teenager is a rollercoaster ride and for the author of this book it's the same just like everyone else, but she ignited her true essence at a young age and thought to share her glimmer and sparkles through this book. Priyal has been a very keen observer and noted all that came her way. Gratitude and love are always found in abundance when one meets her.

Priyal believes in strength and experiencing life through all its endeavours and triumphs. Finding out about every aspect of life, helped her in growing a special fondness for herself.

Living along with the deep essence of Self-Ishq, Turning storms and tornadoes into sunshine and rainbows.

Born in Delhi, Priyal is a very social person and has achieved a lot at a very young age. She has a YouTube channel, The Prisanity, a wonderful page in and out. She is a content writer, loves being a debater, a motivator, public speaker, and counsellor all at the age of 15.

She believes in discovering the creation within, to thrive along the universe by fabricating the elixir of living through spirituality and knowing that you are the one who runs your mind and body. Priyal's mission in life is to live it to the fullest and make everyone do so. She does not see holding any regrets so far in life. With a big bright smile, she moves ahead with pride.

For Priyal, life is learning and teaching experience. This journey has been very sudden and blissful for her just because she knew how to use the power and guidance to its best. In this book she stands by the same by sharing her special secrets and the glow she has through which we all can find the light which is embraced by the darkness within.

Through this book we all can discover our own and very unique radiance.